Challenge able students

Star English

KS3 Classbook

Frank Fitzsimons
Bernadette Tynan

Published by Letts Educational
The Chiswick Centre
414 Chiswick High Road
London W4 5TF

T 020 89963333
F 020 87428390
E mail@lettsed.co.uk
W www.letts-education.com

Letts Educational Limited is a division of Granada Learning Limited, part of Granada plc

First published 2003

ISBN 1 84085 892 3

British Library Cataloguing in Publication Data

A catalogue record for this book is available from the British Library

Developed and packaged by IFA Design Ltd

Commissioned by Helen Clark

Project management by Vicky Butt

Edited by Debbie Pullinger and Rosalind Horton

Cover design by Ken Vail Graphic Design

Cover photo: Tony Stone/Michael Krautwasser

Acknowledgements

The publishers would like to thank the following for permission to use their copyright material. Every effort has been made to trace copyright holders and to obtain their permission for the use of copyright material. The publishers will gladly receive information enabling them to rectify any error or omission in subsequent editions.

p. 6 Extract 'The Gospel of Luke – Chapter 4, verses 1–4, from *The Polyglot Bible*. Reprinted with the kind permission of Mark Davies; p. 46 Extract from *Pygmalion* by George Bernard Shaw. Reprinted with permission of The Society of Authors on behalf of the Bernard Shaw Estate; p. 79 'Who's Who' by W. H. Auden, from *Collected Poems*, published by Faber and Faber. Reprinted with permission of Faber and Faber Limited; p. 82 Extract from 'Afterword: Memorising Poems' by Ted Hughes, from *The Rattle Bag* published by Faber and Faber. Reprinted with permission of Faber and Faber Limited; p. 89 Extract from *A Man For All Seasons* by Robert Bolt. Reprinted with permission of Heinemann part of Harcourt Education Limited; p. 106 'Sacrifice' by Taufiq Rafat, from *Pieces of Eight: Eight Poets From Pakistan* edited by Yuris Said, published by Oxford University Press, Pakistan in 1971. Reprinted with permission of Oxford University Press, Pakistan; p. 108 'Night of the Scorpion' by Nissim Ezekiel, from *Poverty Poems* published by Oxford University Press, India. Reproduced with permission of Oxford University Press, India, New Delhi; p. 110 'Mid Term Break' by Seamus Heaney, from *Death of a Naturalist* published by Faber and Faber. Reprinted with permission of Faber and Faber Limited; p. 117 Extract from *Sahara* by Michael Palin, published by Weidenfeld & Nicholson. © Michael Palin. Reprinted with the kind permission of The Orion Publishing Group and Mayday Management; p. 119 'Quick Balti Sauce' recipe, from *The Complete Cookbook* by Lynette Baxter, published by Bookmart 1994. Copyright © 1994 Bookmart Limited. Reprinted with permission of Bookmart Limited; p. 120 Extracts from an RSPCA appeal leaflet 'will you give an animal the chance this kitten never had' let/78. Reprinted with the kind permission of the RSPCA; p. 122 Extract 'mime' from *Encarta ® World English Dictionary* © & (P) 1999 Microsoft. © Bloomsbury Publishing plc 1999. Reprinted with the kind permission of Bloomsbury Publishing Plc; p. 130 Extract from *Harry Potter and the Philosopher's Stone* by J. K. Rowling. Published by Bloomsbury Publishing Plc. Copyright © J. K. Rowling 1997. Reprinted with the kind permission of The Christopher Little Agency; p. 135 Extract of text and illustrations from Artemis Fowl by Eoin Colfer (Viking 2001) Copyright © Eoin Colfer, 2001. Reprinted with permission of The Penguin Group UK; p. 133 Extract from *A Wizard of Earthsea* by Ursula K. Le Guin. Copyright © 1968, 1996 by the Inter-Vivos Trust for the Le Guin Children. Reprinted by permission of Houghton Mifflin Company. All rights reserved.

Photographs

p. 7 Mary Evans Picture Library; pp. 15, 16 and 176 AKG London; p. 31 Moviestore Collection; pp. 39, 162 and 175 Ronald Grant Archive; p. 42 Kobal Collection (*Pygmalion*), Moviestore Collection (*My Fair Lady*); p. 58 Huntley Film Archives; p. 59 The Dickens House Museum; p. 108 Frank Lane Picture Agency; p. 117 Basil Pao; p. 120 RSPCA Photolibrary.

Illustrations by IFA Design Ltd

Production by PDQ

Printed and bound by Canale, Italy

Contents

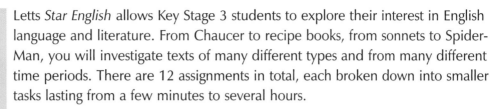

Letts *Star English* allows Key Stage 3 students to explore their interest in English language and literature. From Chaucer to recipe books, from sonnets to Spider-Man, you will investigate texts of many different types and from many different time periods. There are 12 assignments in total, each broken down into smaller tasks lasting from a few minutes to several hours.

Throughout the book you will see a number of symbols. These give information about how best to approach the question being asked.

This symbol means that you should complete the task on your own.

When you see this symbol, you will be working with a partner.

For these questions, you will work in small groups.

This symbol indicates that the whole class will be working together.

The homework symbol indicates questions that could be completed at home.

Information

Information boxes provide additional factual information. For example, they might provide a definition of a new term, or background information on an author or text.

Help

Help boxes provide study tips and guidance. For example, they might suggest tips for giving a presentation, or a way of breaking down a large task.

Resources

Resource boxes provide details of books and websites to help you with your study.

In addition, you will think about *how* you learn: the way you approach tasks, how you work through a problem, how you can improve your results. Ask your teacher to explain these headings:

- ★ *knowledge*
- ★ *comprehension*
- ★ *analysis*
- ★ *application*
- ★ *synthesis*
- ★ *evaluation.*

You will meet these terms throughout *Star English*.

Safety notice!

Whilst Letts has made all reasonable enquiries to ensure all the third party websites listed in this publication and accessible via hyperlinks (or otherwise) are suitable for KS3 students, Letts Educational does not endorse or approve the content of any such third party websites nor does it accept any responsibility or liability for their content. Further, Letts makes no warranty or representation about anything contained in any such third party websites referred to herein or that can be accessed by hyperlink (or otherwise) nor that their URLs will continue to be maintained, available and accessible and accepts no liability in connection with any suggestion or claim that any such third party website breaches any law or regulation or in any other way infringes any of your rights. Also, you acknowledge that internet sites can change very quickly and Letts Educational accepts no responsibility or liability for any subsequent changes to the contents of any such third party websites, their URLs and/or any other online material.

Letts Educational strongly advises teachers, parents and/or guardians to access, review and monitor all such third party websites before directing students to them and also generally for schools actively to encourage parental supervision of students who are accessing the internet at home.

For government guidance on internet safety for schools, please see:
http://safety.ngfl.gov.uk/schools

For government guidance on internet safety for parents, please see:
http://safety.ngfl.gov.uk/parents

The roots of English?

Target

This challenge will enable you to:

* identify the languages that form the roots of English
* discover how and why these key languages influenced English
* appreciate how texts in English changed over time in spelling, phrasing and meaning
* know how to trace the origins of words and explain how their meanings changed over time.

About this assignment

This assignment links to other subjects in the curriculum. Your work may incorporate:

* art
* geography
* ICT (for Internet research)
* music
* drama
* history
* media

Learning styles

For each activity, consider how you might work in the learning style that suits you best:

* auditory
* kinaesthetic
* visual
* any combination of these.

A *What do you know about the English language?*

 45 minutes

knowledge

1 Write down a list of the languages that you think contributed to the English language. *Greek, french, Latin and early Scandinavian.*

2 Briefly explain who brought each language to the British Isles and the activities that they are best known for. You can make linear notes with headings and bullets, or a spidergram.

3 Select a text, such as an article from a newspaper or magazine, and make a list of the ten most frequently used words. Then rank those words in order of frequency. Which language do you think most of them come from?

4 Review your ideas in a whole-class discussion. Compare your lists of top ten words. What kinds of words are they? What is their function in English? Are they adverbs, verbs, adjectives, nouns, prepositions, etc.? Note down any discoveries that you have made. Make a note also of any interesting suggestions that are related to any of the aims of this challenge.

B *Uncover the roots* 2–3 hours

1 Find out more about the peoples and languages that you identified in the first activity. You may add to your list first if you think it is necessary. Focus your research on the following questions:

★ Which English words have been derived from each race or people?

★ What aspect of that people's culture do they emphasise or highlight?

★ What kinds of texts did this people produce, read or listen to? What does this suggest about their culture and their values?

Resources box 1 has some useful websites and books that you can use for your research. Remember also that your library will have books on this topic. Ask your librarian to help you find the resources that you need.

Help

You can write linear notes with headings and bullet points. Or you may prefer to produce a spidergram, or a multiflow map like the one below. Add as many branches as you need.

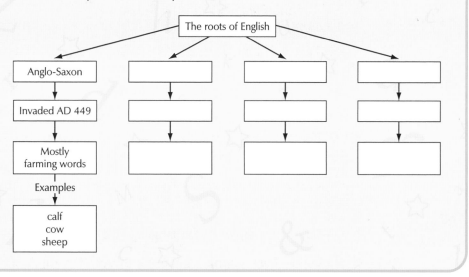

 2 Find a written sample of Old English by looking at the websites or the books in Resources box 1.

Resources 1

For an overview of this topic, visit these sites:

The BBC's *The Anglo-Saxons*
www.bbc.co.uk/education/anglosaxons/index.shtml

Kryss Tal's *The Origin and History of the English Language*
www.krysstal.com/english.html

These sites provide more detailed information:

A (very) brief history of the English Language
http://www.wordorigins.org/histeng.htm

Portus Adurni
http://www9.brinkster.com/saxonshore/portus.asp?Category=ANGLSXNS

Anglo-Saxon heathenism
http://www.englishheathenism.homestead.com/glossary.html

History of English: the key to its spelling
www.unifon.org/history-english.html

You may also find the following books useful if you want to explore the subject in more depth:

The Cambridge Encyclopedia of the English Language by David Crystal, Cambridge University Press (1995)

Word and Phrase Origins by Robert Hendrickson, Facts on File Inc. (2000)

 3

Use your research to produce a timeline that shows how different peoples and races contributed to the development of English up to 1400. Use the following guidelines to help you plan your timeline:

★ Indicate when each race or type of people arrived and their motives for coming to the British Isles.

★ Give a few examples of the language that they brought with them.

★ Show how each people's culture is mirrored in some of the words that they used. For example, the Normans gave English the language of power and government, including words such as *liege* and *royal*.

★ Depict the main images or symbols associated with a race or people.

★ Demonstrate that the development of the English language did not follow a smooth course, for example there was a period of time when English was not spoken at court and was used only by peasants and the uneducated. Show how and when this changed.

★ Give a few examples of words from each language that say the same thing, for example *ask* (Old English), *question* (French) and *interrogate* (Latin). All this, of course, adds to the richness and variety of the English. (Notice that many French words also have their origins in Latin.)

Try to represent your ideas using images and symbols as well as writing. You could even attach objects and artefacts to make your timeline more interesting.

 4

Display all the timelines in a place where they can easily be viewed and discussed. Compare your timeline with the others. Make a note of any insights you gain and any points you want to follow up with other students or your teacher.

As a class, discuss your research and review what you have learned.

Religious texts offer some of the best opportunities to see how Old English developed into modern English. Whereas most texts exist in only one version that reflects the period in which it was written, some religious texts such as the Bible are rewritten and updated over time.

comprehension

1 Look at this extract from the Bible. First read the 1900s version, then compare it with the earlier ones, written in Old English. Look closely at the changes in words and phrasing. Try to work out some of the unfamiliar words in the early texts by comparing them with later versions. (Remember that, over time, the word order would often change too.)

For any words still causing difficulty, see Resources box 2 for sites on Anglo-Saxon.

CH:V	English 1000s	English 1300s	English 1600s	English 1900s
4:1	Soðlice se hælend wæs full halgum gaste and ferde fram iordane. and he wæs fram haligum gaste gelæd. on sumum westene	Forsoþe Jesus ful of þe holi gost, turnede aÿeen fro Jordan, & was led bi þe spirit in to desert	And Jesus being full of the Holy Ghost returned from Jordan, and was led by the Spirit into the wilderness,	Jesus, full of the Holy Spirit, returned from the Jordan and was led by the Spirit in the desert,
4:2	feowertig daga. and wæs fram deofle costod. and he on þam dagum nan þing ne æt; And þam dagum gefylledum hine hingrede;	fourti daÿis, & was temptid bi þe deuel, & eet no þing in þo daÿis, & þo daÿes endid, he hungrede	Being forty days tempted of the devil. And in those days he did eat nothing: and when they were ended, he afterward hungered.	where for forty days he was tempted by the devil. He ate nothing during those days, and at the end of them he was hungry.

continued overleaf

CH:V	English 1000s	English 1300s	English 1600s	English 1900s
4:3	þa cwæð se deofol him to: gif þu sy godes sunu sege þisum stane þæt he to hlafe gewurðe;	forsoþe þe deuel seide to hym, If þou art godis sone, sei to þis ston þat it be maad bred	And the devil said unto him, If thou be the Son of God, command this stone that it be made bread.	The devil said to him, 'If you are the Son of God, tell this stone to become bread.'
4:4	þa andswarude him se hælend; Hit is awriten þæt se man ne leofað be hlafe anum. ac of ælcum godes worde;	& Jesus answerde to hym, It is writen, for a man liueþ not in onli bred, but in euery wrd of god	And Jesus answered him, saying, It is written, That man shall not live by bread alone, but by every word of God.	Jesus answered, 'It is written: "Man does not live on bread alone."'

The Gospel of Luke, Chapter 4, verses 1–4
From *The Polyglot Bible*, Mark Davies
mdavies.for.ilstu.edu/bible/

Resources 2

For a glossary of Anglo-Saxon words:

http://freepages.education.rootsweb.com/~kallenbach/Anglo_Saxon_Glossary.htm

For a Modern English to Old English vocabulary list:

http://www.mun.ca/Ansaxdat/vocab/wordlist.html#s

For help with Anglo-Saxon spelling:

History of English: The key to its spelling
http://www.unifon.org/history-english.html

To hear how Old English sounded when spoken aloud:

The Lord's Prayer in Old English: Matthew, Chapter 6, verses 9–13.
http://www.georgetown.edu/cball/oe/paternoster-oe.html

2 Here are some questions to help you continue your study of these Bible texts, which can be done on your own or in pairs. You do not have to answer every question, but make sure that your research includes some work at each level. If further issues and questions arise as you go along, note them down and try to find out about these too.

Your answers can be in whatever form best suits you and is appropriate for the questions. You could produce linear notes, spidergrams, bubble diagrams with images, or, for some sentence-level and word-level questions, you might find it easiest to make a chart.

Text level

✦ What kind of a text is this and why was it rewritten in each period?

✦ What was the purpose of this text?

✦ Who would have read this text and who would have listened to it?

✦ What was the level of literacy in the population up to 1600?

✦ Who would have commissioned each new version of this text and how would it have been made?

✦ Why would this text have been expensive to produce?

✦ For some years after 1066, the Bible would not have been written in English. Who wrote the first English translation after this period and when did he do so? How was it received?

✦ Find a page of the Bible at the British Library's website – look at Resources box 3. What does its appearance say about its value as a text and as a work of art for people in the Middle Ages?

A 13th-century English Bible. The writing and the detailed artwork would all have been produced by hand.

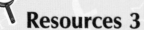

Resources 3

To see a page of Bible manuscript:

The British Library – The Sherborne Missal
http://www.bl.uk/collections/treasures/missal.html

For some background information on illuminated manuscripts:

Medieval writing
http://medievalwriting.50megs.com/

Sentence level

✦ Look carefully at one or two verses and examine any changes in the words and phrases that show changes in language and perhaps culture. Remember that translators translate for meaning and not word for word or phrase for phrase. For instance, in verse 4 the Old English adverb 'forsooth' was not used in the versions from 1600 and 1900; the meaning of this emphatic word seems to be conveyed in the later translations through the general tone.

✦ Do some verses show any variations in tone between versions?

✦ Look at the variation in length. Which versions are most concise and why do you think this is?

✦ Which versions do you prefer and why?

Word level

✦ Select a few words that have been used in each translation and examine how the letters and spelling changed over time. Are there any similarities in how words changed? What has been dropped and what added?

✦ What patterns of language can you establish?

✦ What words seem to stand out and why do you think that they do?

✦ Identify three or four words that are present in each text and explain their importance.

✦ Do the sounds of the words matter? For example, are some words hard and some soft? Do they set a tone?

✦ Is it possible to establish the audience's expectations from the words and phrases in some sections?

synthesis

3 Spend a few minutes going over your work in pairs, according to how you worked during this activity. Go through your notes and ideas so you will be able to talk about some of them in a whole-class discussion. Think also about the following questions:

★ Have you any further questions on this topic?

★ Which questions did you think were most and least relevant?

★ Are there aspects of the topic that still puzzle you?

★ Which parts of the activity did you learn most from?

Asking questions is part of the self-regulatory learning process called metacognition: 'thinking about thinking'. Are you *thinking* enough about what and how you learn?

evaluation

4 As a class, talk about some of the questions set for this activity and discuss any further questions that were raised. Update your notes and answers in the light of new insights or information. Make a note also of areas for further questions and research.

D *Word search* *2–3 hours*

application

1 Your task is to select a word from the *Oxford English Dictionary* and give a presentation to the class on the origins of this word and how it has changed, helped form other words, or gathered new meaning over time.

★ Aim to choose a word that you think is culturally important, because this will inspire you to give a better presentation. Your word does not need to be very old. Over centuries, new words and phrases from many races and cultures have entered the English language – making it a language that is living and growing. The list below gives some examples of interesting words that are well worth researching. You could choose one of these or you could find another word.

charity	common	consume	create
culture	democratic	family	fiction
genius	history	image	literature
myth	nature	private	science
society	taste	wealth	work

* You will need to use the *Oxford English Dictionary* for your research. You could also use other dictionaries that give the etymologies (origins) of words. Your first port of call ought to be your library. You will also find a number of helpful books and websites in Resources box 4.

* As you carry out your research, prepare your notes in the way that best suits your learning style, for example linear notes with headings, spidergrams, or flowcharts.

* If you find that you do not have enough material for one word you could always prepare a presentation for two or three words.

Help

Think about the best ways of presenting your research to your audience. Try to find a way of using your own learning style in your presentation as well as taking account of other students' learning styles. You could present your work as:

* a song – pop, rock, traditional or rap

* a large, colourful visual display that you can talk about

* a talk with a PowerPoint presentation

* a story (telling the story of the word)

* a drama or mime in which you personify the word

* a formal talk

* a taped interview for a radio programme on the English language

* a videotaped interview for a television programme on the origins of words

* a website projected on a whiteboard which you can demonstrate as you talk.

Or you may have other ideas for presenting your ideas in an effective, interesting and memorable way.

You could prepare your talk with basic points on cards the size of postcards.

Do not write too much on the cards and make sure that your writing is big enough to read easily. Alternatively, you could prepare a colourful spidergram with strong images depicting each new stage in your talk.

Your teacher will give you an annotated example of an entry from a dictionary to help you see how information is presented for each word.

Resources 4

Advice and links on how to read and understand word entries in the *Oxford English Dictionary* (The OED) can be found at:
http://dictionary.oed.com/public/help/OED_guide/overview.htm
http://dictionary.oed.com/public/help/OED_guide/

Better Editor Org. – Etymology, Dictionaries and Resources
http://bettereditor.org/resources/dictionaries/etymology_dictionaries.htm

Focusing On Words (Latin and Greek Words)
http://www.wordfocus.com/

Wilton's Word and Phrase Origins
http://www.wordorigins.org/index.htm

For language varieties and dialects from around the world see:
http://www.une.edu.au/langnet/

The Cambridge Encyclopedia of the English Language by David Crystal, Cambridge University Press (1995)

E *Learning review*

30 minutes

evaluation

 1 Review your presentation and think about how successful you have been in communicating your learning to your peers. What did you do well and what could you have done better? Write a few notes on how things turned out, then fill in the assessment grid.

 How confident are you that you achieved the aims of this challenge?

Aim achieved	Not very confident	Reasonably confident	Confident	Very confident
I identified the main languages that form the roots of English.				
I discovered how and why these key languages influenced English.				

continued overleaf

Aim achieved	Not very confident	Reasonably confident	Confident	Very confident
I can appreciate how texts in English changed over time in spelling, phrasing and meaning.				
I know how to trace the origins of words and explain how their meanings changed over time.				

Go over any aims where you still lack confidence by doing further research and by talking to students and teachers.

evaluation

 2

Consider also *how* you learned during this assignment. Use the checklist below to assess your skills as an independent learner. What were the skills that you developed? What skills do you need to develop further?

A checklist of intrapersonal study skills

✦ I showed good or excellent interpersonal skills when I worked in pairs, or groups or with the whole class.

✦ My research skills have improved through my familiarity with the Internet or libraries.

✦ I used my learning style effectively during this assignment.

✦ I showed creative flair and ability during this assignment.

✦ I worked in a flexible way.

✦ I was able to integrate new ideas in my work.

✦ I showed persistence as I worked steadily towards the main aims of this challenge.

✦ I returned to ideas that I did not understand and found new or different answers for them.

✦ I was able to accept different interpretations and ideas made by other students and can acknowledge diversity.

★ I discovered some unusual ideas and information during my research.

★ I gained confidence in myself as an independent learner.

★ I showed energy and commitment during this challenge.

★ I reflected on what I knew and used metacognition when I needed to.

Write down any other further points that you would like to make about your level of study skills?

If you did not agree with every point on the checklist, briefly state what happened. Then make a note of any study skills targets that you wish to achieve in your next challenge.

Resources 5

Find out more about intrapersonal intelligence and the other intelligences that make up the set of multiple intelligences by visiting this website:

The Gardner School
http://www.gardnerschool.org/multiple_intelligences.html

3 Keep all the notes, brainstorms and work produced during this assignment in a portfolio that you and your teacher can review when you have finished. Keeping a portfolio is useful because you can use it to check your progress later in the school term or year.

Next steps

Find out more about the cultural diversity of English and discover how this diversity grew through the growth of the British Empire and other cultural influences over time.

Target

This challenge will enable you to:

★ understand Chaucer's 'General Prologue' in *The Canterbury Tales*

★ find out what medieval pilgrims were like and understand why they went on pilgrimage

★ appreciate how Chaucer's first-person narrator portrays pilgrims through speech and skilful description

★ determine which characters attract least and most criticism and justify your conclusions

★ come to a judgement on which of Chaucer's pilgrims is the most interesting.

Other significant aims in this challenge include:

★ establishing Chaucer's purpose for writing his 'General Prologue'

★ understanding how Chaucer uses language to create a range of meaning

★ gaining an appreciation of how the pronunciation of words has changed over time

★ understanding how words have accrued various meanings over time.

About this assignment

This assignment links to other subjects in the curriculum. Your work may incorporate:

★ drama   ★ history (Medieval)

★ ICT (for Internet research)   ★ media

★ music

Learning styles

For each activity, consider how you might work in the learning style that suits you best:

★ auditory   ★ kinaesthetic   ★ visual   ★ any combination of these.

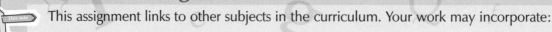

A   *Pilgrimage to Canterbury* 60–90 minutes

knowledge

1   Find out about Thomas Becket and why his shrine at Canterbury was such a popular place of pilgrimage until the early 1500s. As you gather information, focus on the following questions:

Sir Thomas Becket is consecrated Archbishop of Canterbury in 1162. From the *Queen Mary Psalter*, a 13th-century illuminated manuscript.

✴ What are the main facts surrounding Becket's life and death?

✴ Why was pilgrimage important during the Middle Ages?

✴ Why would pilgrims have gone to visit Becket's shrine at Canterbury?

✴ What types of people would have been pilgrims and what were their reasons for going?

✴ What costs and risks were involved in going on pilgrimage?

✴ Which were the important pilgrimage routes in Britain and Europe?

✴ What was life usually like for pilgrims on pilgrimage?

You can search for information using encyclopaedias and the library as well as the websites in Resources box 1.

This background knowledge will help you gain a deeper insight into the pilgrims that Chaucer describes in his 'General Prologue' to his *Canterbury Tales*. Chaucer's characters may have been stereotypes to a degree, but they were almost certainly drawn from Chaucer's own experience as a traveller and as a pilgrim.

Summarise what you found out in notes so that you can give feedback in a whole-class discussion. You could make linear notes with headings and bullet points, or a spidergram. Or you could try a circle map diagram, like this one, to organise your ideas on the life and death of Becket.

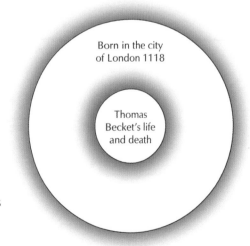

Born in the city of London 1118

Thomas Becket's life and death

Resources 1

http://icg.fas.harvard.edu/~chaucer/

http://www.cas.suffolk.edu/english/richman/Eng323/intro.htm

http://www.historylearningsite.co.uk/becket.htm

http://crusades.boisestate.edu/vpilgrim/Background/pilgrimage.htm

http://faculty.stcc.cc.tn.us/bmcclure/Links/canterbury.htm

For more information on the Middle Ages see:

http://radiantworks.com/middleages/

evaluation

   2

Use your notes to help you make points in a whole-class discussion. During the discussion, listen for any points that further your understanding of Chaucer's pilgrims and add them to your notes.

B — *Chaucer introduces the pilgrims*   *90 minutes*

knowledge

   1

On your own or in pairs, read this opening passage from the 'General Prologue' two or three times. Auditory learners may prefer to read these lines as Chaucer most probably intended, aloud. Tactile learners could pick up the book and pace the room as they read. You should not expect to understand challenging texts like this on a first reading. To help you interpret the 14th-century language and spellings, a modern translation has been provided alongside the original.

The Knight, the Squire and the Prioress from *The Canterbury Tales* (an 1868 woodcut based on the 15th-century Ellesmere manuscript).

The Canterbury Tales : General Prologue

Here bygynneth the Book of the tales of Caunterbury

Here begins the Book of the Tales of Canterbury

1: Whan that Aprill with his shoures soote	When April with his showers sweet with fruit
2: The droghte of March hath perced to the roote,	The drought of March has pierced unto the root
3: And bathed every veyne in swich licour	And bathed each vein with liquor that has power
4: Of which vertu engendred is the flour;	To generate therein and sire the flower;
5: Whan Zephirus eek with his sweete breeth	When Zephyr also has, with his sweet breath,
6: Inspired hath in every holt and heeth	Quickened again, in every holt and heath,
7: The tendre croppes, and the yonge sonne	The tender shoots and buds, and the young sun
8: Hath in the Ram his half cours yronne,	Into the Ram one half his course has run,
9: And smale foweles maken melodye,	And many little birds make melody
10: That slepen al the nyght with open ye	That sleep through all the night with open eye
11: (So priketh hem nature in hir corages),	(So Nature pricks them on to ramp and rage) –
12: Thanne longen folk to goon on pilgrimages,	Then do folk long to go on pilgrimage,
13: And palmeres for to seken straunge strondes,	And palmers to go seeking out strange strands,
14: To ferne halwes, kowthe in sondry londes;	To distant shrines well known in sundry lands.
15: And specially from every shires ende	And specially from every shire's end
16: Of Engelond to Caunterbury they wende,	Of England they to Canterbury wend,
17: The hooly blisful martir for to seke,	The holy blessed martyr there to seek
18: That hem hath holpen whan that they were seeke.	Who helped them when they lay so ill and weak
19: Bifil that in that seson on a day,	Befell that, in that season, on a day
20: In Southwerk at the Tabard as I lay	In Southwark, at the Tabard, as I lay
21: Redy to wenden on my pilgrymage	Ready to start upon my pilgrimage
22: To Caunterbury with ful devout corage,	To Canterbury, full of devout homage,
23: At nyght was come into that hostelrye	There came at nightfall to that hostelry
24: Wel nyne and twenty in a compaignye	Some nine and twenty in a company
25: Of sondry folk, by aventure yfalle	Of sundry persons who had chanced to fall
26: In felaweshipe, and pilgrimes were they alle,	In fellowship, and pilgrims were they all
27: That toward Caunterbury wolden ryde.	That toward Canterbury town would ride.
28: The chambres and the stables weren wyde,	The rooms and stables spacious were and wide,
29: And wel we weren esed atte beste.	And well we there were eased, and of the best.
30: And shortly, whan the sonne was to reste,	And briefly, when the sun had gone to rest,
31: So hadde I spoken with hem everichon	So had I spoken with them, every one,
32: That I was of hir felaweshipe anon,	That I was of their fellowship anon,
33: And made forward erly for to ryse,	And made agreement that we'd early rise
34: To take oure wey ther as I yow devyse.	To take the road, as you I will apprise.
35: But nathelees, whil I have tyme and space,	But none the less, whilst I have time and space,

36: Er that I ferther in this tale pace,	Before yet farther in this tale I pace,
37: Me thynketh it acordaunt to resoun	It seems to me accordant with reason
38: To telle yow al the condicioun	To inform you of the state of every one
39: Of ech of hem, so as it semed me,	Of all of these, as it appeared to me,
40: And whiche they weren, and of what degree,	And who they were, and what was their degree,
41: And eek in what array that they were inne;	And even how arrayed there at the inn;
42: And at a knyght than wol I first bigynne.	And with a knight thus will I first begin.

The Canterbury Tales, 'The General Prologue', Lines 1–42
From *Medieval Sourcebook: Geoffrey Chaucer*
The Canterbury Tales: Prologue Parallel Texts
http://www.fordham.edu/halsall/source/CT-prolog-para.html

---

comprehension

2 As you study this passage, make brief notes (linear notes or a spidergram) to answer the questions below.

Text level

✶ Sum up in one or two paragraphs what Chaucer is saying in this extract. For instance, what motivates the narrator and others to go on pilgrimage? This will help you to understand what Chaucer was setting out to achieve in the introduction to his 'General Prologue'.

✶ In Chaucer's time, people lived their lives by the seasons much more than we do today. Why does Chaucer's narrator choose spring as a symbolically significant time to go on pilgrimage?

✶ What kind of narrator is speaking in this extract and why is such a narrator suitable for the prologue?

✶ William Caxton's printing press was still several decades away, so Chaucer's texts would have been laboriously and expensively copied by hand. What kinds of books do you think were the most frequently copied in Chaucer's time? (One of the websites given for researching Becket may help you with this question.)

✶ The narrator seems pleased to meet such a large number of pilgrims and to join them at the tavern. What were the benefits and disadvantages for pilgrims of travelling in large groups on the road to their destination?

synthesis

3 In a group of four to six students, discuss your answers to the text-level questions. Add to your notes any interesting new points from others' contributions.

Help

Group organisation

Your group will need to choose:

- ★ a chairperson to manage contributions from group members
- ★ a recorder to note the main points and answers agreed by the group
- ★ a spokesperson for feeding back your ideas to the whole class.

Roles should be alternated in future group sessions so that everyone gets the experience of playing a different role within a group. Each role needs to be carefully defined. The chairperson, for instance, will need to ensure that each group member gets a chance to speak and that everyone else listens to their ideas and views.

evaluation

 4

For each question, the spokesperson from each group should give feedback in turn. For some questions, it may be helpful to discuss points and ideas arising out of the feedback, especially if groups have varying or different answers.

Again, add to your personal notes any fresh points of interest arising out of the general discussion.

C How was Chaucer's text read?

90 minutes

analysis

 1

Here are some questions to help you continue your study of Chaucer's 'General Prologue', which can be done on your own or in pairs. Your answers can be in whatever form best suits you and is appropriate for the questions. You could produce linear notes, spidergrams or bubble diagrams with images.

Sentence level

★ Do you think Chaucer wrote his *Canterbury Tales* to be read privately by individuals or to be performed from memory by a storyteller in a social setting, such as a house, tavern or hall? Consider the reasons for each possibility by looking again at the original text and its rhythm and rhyme. Kinaesthetic learners may prefer to tap or sound out the rhythm of syllables as they work out each line's rhythm. Note how the rhythm of each line rises and falls with the sounds of each word.

✦ How does the form or appearance of Chaucer's text differ from texts from later centuries? Why do you think Chaucer set down his poem line after line without any breaks or spaces at all? Speculate on the advantages and disadvantages of setting out a text in this way.

Word level

✦ What has happened to spelling since the 1400s? Choose around ten words from the extract from Chaucer's prologue and compare them with modern spellings, looking at the similarities and differences. What letters have been dropped or changed? Suggest some possible reasons for the changes.

✦ Look at how vowels are used. What are the implications for how Old English was pronounced?

✦ Find out about the 'great vowel shift'. What happened to the sounds people made as they pronounced and articulated their words? Go to the two websites in Resources box 2 for help with this task.

✦ No one really knows why the great vowel shift took place, but you might like to speculate about possible reasons!

Resources 2

The Geoffrey Chaucer Page: The Great Vowel Shift
http://icg.fas.harvard.edu/~chaucer/vowels.html

The Great Vowel Shift
http://alpha.furman.edu/~mmenzer/gvs/seehear.htm

The English Language by David Crystal, Penguin Books (2002)

A History of the English Language by Thomas Cable and Albert C. Baugh, Routledge – an imprint of Taylor and Francis Books Ltd (2002)

evaluation

2   Compare your answers in a whole-class discussion. Again, modify your answers and notes if you need to, adding any new and interesting points.

D   *Analyse one of Chaucer's characters*    90 minutes

comprehension

1   One of the pilgrims in *The Canterbury Tales* is a miller. Read the description of the Miller, then work on your own or with a partner to answer the following questions:

★ From your first reading, how do you think this pilgrim's character is portrayed?

★ Now reread the description carefully and make notes on what the narrator says about the Miller, for example on several lines the narrator suggests that the Miller is a strong rogue (stout churl). Some of what he says is implied rather than stated. So think carefully about the symbolic association of the colours of the Miller's clothes, his actions and his appearance.

★ Decide whether the narrator portrays the Miller in a positive or negative way and give reasons for your decision.

Your teacher may give out an enlarged copy of this text so that you can annotate it as a record of your findings.

The Miller's Portrait

545: The Millere was a stout carl for the nones;
546: Ful byg he was of brawn, and eek of bones.
547: That proved wel, for over al ther he cam,
548: At wrastlynge he wolde have alwey the ram.
549: He was short-sholdred, brood, a thikke knarre;
550: Ther was no dore that he nolde heve of harre,
551: Or breke it at a rennyng with his heed.
552: His berd as any sowe or fox was reed,
553: And therto brood, as though it were a spade.
554: Upon the cop right of his nose he hade
555: A werte, and theron stood a toft of herys,
556: Reed as the brustles of a sowes erys;
557: His nosethirles blake were and wyde.
558: A swerd and bokeler bar he by his syde.
559: His mouth as greet was as a greet forneys.
560: He was a janglere and a goliardeys,
561: And that was moost of synne and harlotries.
562: Wel koude he stelen corn and tollen thries;
563: And yet he hadde a thombe of gold, pardee.
564: A whit cote and a blew hood wered he.
565: A baggepipe wel koude he blowe and sowne,
566: And therwithal he broghte us out of towne.

THE MILLER

The miller was a stout churl, be it known,
Hardy and big of brawn and big of bone;
Which was well proved, for when he went on lam
At wrestling, never failed he of the ram.
He was a chunky fellow, broad of build;
He'd heave a door from hinges if he willed,
Or break it through, by running, with his head.
His beard, as any sow or fox, was red,
And broad it was as if it were a spade.
Upon the coping of his nose he had
A wart, and thereon stood a tuft of hairs,
Red as the bristles in an old sow's ears;
His nostrils they were black and very wide.
A sword and buckler bore he by his side.
His mouth was like a furnace door for size.
He was a jester and could poetize,
But mostly all of sin and ribaldries.
He could steal corn and full thrice charge his fees;
And yet he had a thumb of gold, begad.
A white coat and blue hood he wore, this lad.
A bagpipe he could blow well, be it known,
And with that same he brought us out of town.

The Canterbury Tales, 'The General Prologue', Lines 545–566
From *Medieval Sourcebook: Geoffrey Chaucer*
The Canterbury Tales: Prologue Parallel Texts
http://www.fordham.edu/halsall/source/CT-prolog-para.html

Information

physiognomy: the art of judging a person's character from the features of the face or the form of the body.

It was commonplace in Chaucer's time to believe that a person's face and build could act as a guide to their character. Chaucer's narrator often uses physiognomy as a sort of shorthand to suggest character traits for the pilgrims. The descriptions draw upon stereotypes which a contemporary audience of *The Canterbury Tales* would easily identify and understand.

Chaucer's narrator (a pilgrim called Chaucer) deliberately exaggerates the facial and bodily features of the Miller so that he has the look and build of a strong, prosperous peasant. He is rough, round and ruddy; he has a big mouth and a wart on his nose. His appearance fits the stereotype peasant of his time. His behaviour, motives and actions can also be inferred from his appearance.

Stereotypes are often used today for similar reasons. Advertisers rely on stereotypes to save time and money in commercials. They present characters that conform to their audience's expectations of how a particular type of person is expected to dress, look and behave. For instance, a judge in adverts is invariably a serious old man who peers over his glasses at members of the court of whom he disapproves; he will often seem slightly out of touch and have an upper crust accent. The advertisement producer may then play with this stereotype to help make a product more memorable for consumers. For example, the judge may break expected conventions by losing his serious appearance and doing a tap dance – after eating or drinking the product being advertised!

Resources 3

For help with your investigation into Chaucer's text, have a look at this website, which has a glossary of frequently used words from Chaucer as well as a section on pronunciation.

http://icg.fas.harvard.edu/~chaucer/pronunciation/

2   If you have not done so already, pair up with another student and compare your answers to the questions on the Miller in question 1. Consider also the following questions.

✦ Is Chaucer's narrator (also called Chaucer) an objective or a subjective narrator? In other words, can he be relied upon to give an unbiased account of his fellow pilgrims?

✦ Why do you think that Chaucer felt it was necessary to create a narrator in the tales with his own name?

✦ Do you think that Chaucer sometimes plays with his audience's expectations of his pilgrims? Have the pilgrims you have studied differed from their stereotypes in any meaningful way?

evaluation

 3

Compare your views and ideas in a whole-class discussion. Remember to update your notes and answers with any new and interesting points. Write down any ideas that you need to follow up with further research.

E *Compare Chaucer's characterisations* *3 hours*

analysis

 1

Your task is to do an in-depth study of Chaucer's characterisation in the 'General Prologue' and to compare the way the different pilgrims are portrayed. Choose *one* of these two questions, then use the guidelines below to organise your research.

✦ Which pilgrims do you think attract the least and most criticism from the narrator in the 'General Prologue'? Explain the reasons for your choices.

✦ Which pilgrims in the 'General Prologue' are the most interesting and why?

Resources 4

Your teacher may supply you with a copy of the 'General Prologue'. Alternatively you can find the original and translated texts alongside each other on the following websites:

Medieval Sourcebook: Geoffrey Chaucer, d. 1400: Canterbury Tales: Prologue [Parallel Texts]
http://www.fordham.edu/halsall/source/CT-prolog-para.html

The Geoffrey Chaucer Page
http://icg.fas.harvard.edu/~chaucer/teachslf/gp-par.htm

If you would like the challenge of reading Chaucer's original text, you will need a good glossary. An extensive one can be found at:
http://www.librarius.com/cantales.htm

Help

First impressions

In your first reading of the 'General Prologue', try to get an impression of what each pilgrim's character is like and make some brief notes. Auditory learners could read the text aloud, just as Chaucer had probably intended. In fact, criticism and approval may be noticed more easily when the text is read aloud.

Some of the narrator's criticisms of the pilgrims will be overt although many more will be ironic and therefore implied. Keep a sharp look out for both types and be prepared to weigh the critical comments made about each pilgrim against positive ones. (If you are not sure about the meaning of irony, check it in a dictionary.)

Character studies

Now carefully reread the description of each pilgrim. Make notes on each one (linear or spidergram) using the questions below:

Your teacher will give you a chart to fill in if you would rather record your points and ideas in that format.

- ⭐ What can be drawn from each pilgrim's physiognomy (character as suggested by appearance)?

- ⭐ Can any inferences be made from their speech or their topics of conversation?

- ⭐ What do they do and how do they act? Is this always in keeping with their status or professed trade?

- ⭐ What are their inner motives?

- ⭐ How do they get on with other characters? Is there any friction between them? What do they really think of each other?

- ⭐ Can any symbolic associations be drawn from a character's clothes or from colours used in their description?

- ⭐ Are they compared with birds or animals? Look for any telling similes or metaphors and make a note of any deeper meanings that can be drawn from such comparisons.

- ⭐ Do they have any props or instruments and what do these imply about the character?

Review

Now look again at the text as a whole alongside your character studies. Consider and make notes on the following questions:

- ⭐ Looking at his overt and implied comments for each pilgrim, what does Chaucer's narrator think of them? How is the audience guided in its thoughts about the characters?

* Can anything be inferred from the order in which Chaucer places his pilgrims in the prologue? Has this anything to do with a character's status, for example? Do you think their order of appearance is random or deliberate? Give a reason for your answer.

* Make a final judgement on whether you think the narrator portrays each character in a positive or negative way. Try to give at least one quotation in your notes to support your judgement.

Remember that as well as setting the scene, 'The General Prologue' is intended to introduce each pilgrim to Chaucer's audience. Later, in the main body of *The Canterbury Tales*, each pilgrim tells their own tale and becomes the main narrator for a time. The main narrator then acts as an intermediary, linking the tales.

Resources 5

Interesting comments on some of the pilgrims can be found at this webpage that cites an extract from Brother Anthony's *Literature in English Society: The Middle Ages*:

http://ccsun7.sogang.ac.kr/~anthony/Chaucer/Genprol.htm

synthesis

 2

Now go through your notes and decide how you will answer the question that you selected at the beginning of the task. Take your time as you do this because you will need to reflect on your findings and think carefully about them before you make any judgements

If you chose the first question, consider also:

★ your gut feelings about the characters

★ the moral case for each one

★ which characters you empathise with least and most.

If you chose the second question, the notes you made for the character studies will form the basis of your decisions.

You will also need to think about evidence (including brief quotations) that you could use in a whole-class discussion to support your ideas about your chosen characters.

application

1 Using all the notes you made in the previous task, prepare a presentation of your ideas for the whole class. Be prepared to defend your choice of pilgrims in a question-and-answer session afterwards.

Here are just a few of the ways that you could present your ideas in a way that best suits your strongest learning style. By working to your strengths you will also be in a better position to engage and hold your classmates' interest and attention.

Visual-linguistic

Visual-linguistic learners love reading and writing and enjoy manipulating language in a creative and expressive way. If this is your preferred learning style, you could:

★ give a PowerPoint presentation on your chosen character(s)

★ give a 'point-and-talk' presentation using an annotated copy of the character's description displayed on an overhead projector

★ write a letter to the character from an admirer or foe, and read it to the class

★ write a poem on the traits of your chosen characters

★ use a flipchart to take the class through your main ideas.

Visual-spatial

Visual-spatial learners have strong visual imaginations and they are good at anything to do with pattern and design. They are great at expressing their moods, thoughts and feelings through images. If this is your preferred learning style, you could:

★ create a poster or a display that justifies your choice of characters. Explain its details and images and any props or items that you have attached to it

★ create a colourful spidergram with images that shows details of your judgement on your chosen character(s)

★ give a talk using flashcards and props associated with your chosen characters.

Kinaesthetic

Kinaesthetic learners love to move around and use their hands to manipulate objects or use their natural balance in any activity to do with movement. If this is your preferred learning style, you could:

★ create a role-play for your selected character(s)

★ create a mime that expresses the chosen characters through movement

★ create a dance for your characters and then explain the significance of steps and movement and what they imply.

Auditory

Auditory learners are often musically minded or like to verbalise their learning. If this is your preferred learning style, you could:

★ make a taped or videotaped interview of the character in a chat show

★ compose a song or songs that justifies your choice of character(s)

★ put yourself as the character in the 'hot seat' and invite your knowledgeable audience to ask you questions on why you are the most interesting, or most or least criticised of Chaucer's pilgrims.

You can, of course, do a variation on any of these ideas, or agree a completely different activity with your teacher. What matters is that you explain and give evidence for your decisions and are able to justify your choice of pilgrim when fielding questions from your classmates after your presentation.

evaluation

2 Review your work as a class. Consider any new insights or changes of mind that may have resulted from learning about each other's choices of characters and the evidence and reasoning behind them. As a class you could consider:

★ why some characters were a popular choice

★ why other characters were not a popular choice

★ whether, as a class, you can agree 'the most interesting' or the 'least criticised' and 'most criticised' characters

★ whether some students have now changed their minds about their original choices, having been persuaded by other presentations

★ what you learned from having to defend and justify your choices

★ what you discovered about Chaucer's pilgrims that you did not know before.

Share your new knowledge with a wider audience. You could pool your resources and produce a display on Chaucer's pilgrims for a classroom, main corridor, or a special display for an open evening in your school.

A group or class display would allow the class to develop its interpersonal intelligence as you share roles and work together as a team to show what you have learned. If you do this, remember to ask those with visual-spatial intelligence for advice on the design and layout of your display!

evaluation

 1 Think about your own achievements and successes in this assignment.

Write a few notes on how things turned out, then fill in the assessment grid.

How confident are you that you achieved the main aims of this challenge? (For the last two rows, fill in only the one that applies.)

Aim achieved	Not very confident	Reasonably confident	Confident	Very confident
I understand the 'General Prologue'.				
I found out what medieval pilgrims were like.				
I appreciate speech and skilful description by Chaucer's first person narrator.				
I identified characters most and least criticised.				
I judged the most interesting pilgrims.				

How confident are you that you achieved the other significant aims of this challenge? (For the last two rows, fill in only the one that applies.)

Aim achieved	Not very confident	Reasonably confident	Confident	Very confident
I established Chaucer's purpose for writing his 'General Prologue'.				
I know how Chaucer used language to create a range of meaning.				

Aim achieved	Not very confident	Reasonably confident	Confident	Very confident
I appreciate how the pronunciation has changed over time.				
I understand that words have accrued various meanings over time.				

What else did you learn during the course of this assignment?

Do you need to revisit any part of this assignment to strengthen your understanding? Rather than rushing on to the next assignment it is always worth securing your knowledge by going over anything that you may not have fully understood. Make sure that the foundations of your skills and knowledge are solid before you build on them.

Next steps

Why not read the tale of one or more of your chosen pilgrims. Whichever tale you read, consider how the content of the story suits the character of its teller.

Resources 6

Several of the websites that you may have already visited will have links to copies of *The Canterbury Tales*. Here are a couple of others you may like to try.

An excellent website where you can see and hear a BBC cartoon version of 'The Nun's Priest's Tale':
http://news.bbc.co.uk/1/hi/entertainment/the_oscars_1999/297262.stm

For the 'General Prologue' and readings of some of the tales:
http://www.unc.edu/depts/chaucer/chworks.htm

Click on the underlined titles that are shown with line numbers. You could follow the readings with the text in front of you.

Target

This challenge will enable you to:

★ identify each of Shakespeare's three styles of language: prose, blank verse and rhymed verse

★ understand why Shakespeare selected each style of language for his characters

★ analyse and appreciate blank verse and rhyming couplets.

About this assignment

This assignment links to other subjects in the curriculum. Your work may incorporate:

★ dance
★ drama
★ history
★ ICT (for Internet research)
★ media
★ music

Learning styles

For each activity, consider how you might work in the learning style that suits you best:

★ auditory
★ kinaesthetic
★ visual
★ any combination of these.

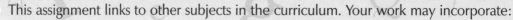

A *Do you know Shakespeare?*

10 minutes

knowledge

1 Write down five things that you know about Shakespeare – the man and his plays. (Visual learners may prefer to make a spidergram.)

2 Write down up to five things that you know about the play *Romeo and Juliet*.

synthesis

3 Share your lists with a partner and discuss what you already know about Shakespeare and *Romeo and Juliet*.

knowledge

1 Read the extracts below from the play *Romeo and Juliet* by William Shakespeare.

Leonardo di Caprio as Romeo in the 1996 film version of *Romeo and Juliet* directed by Baz Luhrmann.

Romeo Montague and his friend Benvolio learn by chance of 'an ancient feast' hosted by their bitter rivals, the Capulets. Romeo reluctantly decides to gatecrash this feast. He goes partly because he may see Rosaline, the young Capulet woman who spurned him, and partly at the insistence of Benvolio, who gives Romeo the age-old advice that 'there are other fish in the sea'.

Extract 1

BENVOLIO	At this same ancient feast of Capulet's
[To Romeo]	Sups the fair Rosaline, whom thou so loves,
	With all the admired beauties of Verona.
	Go thither and with unattained eye
	Compare her face with some that I shall show
	And I will make thee think thy swan a crow.

Romeo and Juliet, Act 1, scene 2, lines 84–89

The Capulets' servants are busy preparing for the family's feast.

Extract 2

1 SERVINGMAN	You are looked for and called for, asked
	for and sought for, in the great chamber.

4 SERVINGMAN	We cannot be here and there too.
	Cheerly, boys! Be brisk awhile, and the longer liver
	take all.*

Romeo and Juliet, Act 1, scene 5, lines 12–15

Once at the feast, it does not take long for Romeo to spot Juliet.

ROMEO	[To a servant] What lady's that which doth enrich the
	hand
	Of yonder knight?

| SERVANT | I know not, sir. |

ROMEO	[To himself] O, she doth teach the torches to burn bright.
	It seems she hangs upon the cheek of night
	As a rich jewel in an Ethiop's ear –
	Beauty too rich for use, for earth too dear.
	So shows a snowy dove trooping with crows
	As yonder lady o'er her fellows shows.
	The measure done, I'll watch her place of stand,
	And touching hers, make blessed my rude hand.
	Did my heart love till now? Forswear it, sight.
	For I ne'er saw true beauty till this night.

Romeo and Juliet, Act 1, scene 5, lines 42–52

However, the moment that Romeo falls in love is the same moment that he is discovered by Juliet's cousin, the fiery-tempered Tybalt.

TYBALT	This by his voice, should be a Montague.
	Fetch me my rapier, boy. [Exit boy] What, dares the
	slave
	Come hither, cover'd with an antic face,
	To fleer and scorn at our solemnity?
	Now by the stock and honour of my kin,
	To strike him dead I hold it not a sin.

| CAPULET | Why how now kinsman, wherefore storm you so? |

Extract 3

Extract 4

* 'Let the one who lives longest take everything.' This was a popular saying to encourage cheerfulness. It was a common belief that cheerfulness lengthened life.

TYBALT	Uncle, this is a Montague, our foe; A villain that is hither come in spite To scorn at our solemnity this night.
CAPULET	Young Romeo is it?
TYBALT	'Tis he, that villain Romeo.

Romeo and Juliet, Act 1, scene 5, lines 53–64

comprehension

2 Reread the extracts and make notes on the kind of language each character uses. You can make linear notes with headings and bullets, or a spidergram. Identify lines of speech that you think are:

- ★ similar to other lines
- ★ unusual
- ★ striking
- ★ emotional
- ★ poetic
- ★ ordinary.

3 Look over your notes and consider why Shakespeare selects different kinds of speech for his characters.

synthesis

4 Discuss your notes and findings with a partner. What is your most important discovery so far?

evaluation

5 Be prepared to offer points and ideas in a whole-class discussion.

6 Afterwards, add to your notes any interesting or important points that were made during the discussion.

C Rhythm and rhyme

2 hours

knowledge

1 You may have noticed in the extracts from *Romeo and Juliet*, that different characters have different ways of speaking. Now read the following summary of the various types of language used by Shakespeare in his plays.

Information

Shakespeare's three styles of language

Shakespeare uses three main forms of language: prose, blank verse and rhymed verse. In each speech, he selects a form to suit his character's thoughts, feelings and actions.

Prose

Prose is language that has no metrical structure. In other words it does not use poetic rhythm as verse does. In Shakespeare's plays, characters of low social status, such as servants, usually speak in prose, although characters of higher status sometimes speak it too. Shakespeare uses prose for plot development, straightforward information and comic situations. However, there are exceptions, such as when the character Shylock speaks in prose for his heartfelt speech on revenge in *The Merchant of Venice* (Act 3, scene 1, lines 49–67). In his later plays Shakespeare used a greater proportion of prose.

1 SERVINGMAN	You are looked for and called for, asked for and sought for, in the great chamber.
4 SERVINGMAN	We cannot be here and there too.

Romeo and Juliet, Act 1, scene 5, lines 12–14

Blank verse

Blank verse is dramatic and sounds poetic; it is called 'blank' because it does not rhyme. It therefore depends on metre, or rhythm, for its effect. Shakespeare intended this type of verse to represent the rhythms of everyday speech; noble characters use it to show their status, thoughts and feelings. Notice also that both blank verse and rhyming couplets conform to a convention of beginning a new line with a capital letter.

BENVOLIO	At this same ancient feast of Capulet's
	Sups the fair Rosaline, whom thou so loves,
	With all the admired beauties of Verona.
	Go thither and with unattainted eye.

Romeo and Juliet, Act 1, scene 5, lines 84–87

Rhyming couplets

Rhyming couplets also have a metrical structure, but they differ from blank verse in that they rhyme. Rhyming couplets are used during moments of dramatic intensity when characters express strong emotions such as love

and hate. Shakespeare also uses rhyming couplets to signal the departure of characters from the stage as well as the end of scenes and acts. Sometimes it is used within a speech in blank verse to emphasise a character's feelings.

ROMEO   The measure done, I'll watch her place of stand,
         And touching hers, make blessed my rude hand.
         Did my heart love till now? Forswear it, sight,
         For I ne'er saw true beauty till this night.

Romeo and Juliet, Act 1, scene 5, lines 49–52

Notice that Shakespeare elides (from the Latin for 'crushing out') the 'v' from 'never' by substituting an apostrophe in the last line.

evaluation

2 Discuss what you have learned about Shakespeare's three styles of language. Summarise what you have learned in a couple of paragraphs or a spidergram.

D ## Investigate metre

1 hour

analysis

1 Your task is to discover the patterns of rhythm that Shakespeare uses in his verse. Reread the extracts from *Romeo and Juliet* aloud and try to work out which syllables are stressed and which are unstressed. Write down a few well-spaced lines of verse and underscore the stressed syllables with a coloured pen. Then think about the following:

★ What patterns can you establish?

★ Is there a regular syllabic pattern throughout?

★ What units of rhythm can you see?

★ How does the pattern change?

★ Why do you think it changes?

★ What are the rules of writing verse that looks and sounds like this?

★ Make a note of anything that puzzles you so you can ask questions on your points later on.

★ Develop a metrical explanation for 'ne'er' in the line: For I ne'er saw true beauty till this night.

Help

To help you work out the stresses of Shakespeare's verse, try any of the following:

* Throw a tennis ball between you and a partner to emphasise stressed and unstressed syllables as you say the lines aloud.

* Try a musical approach by clapping or beating out each line's rhythm.

* Read the lines as you walk, stamping your feet and changing direction at the end of each line.

Most of Shakespeare's blank verse has a pattern of stressed and unstressed syllables called 'iambic pentameter'. Find out what this term means. The sound is 'ti-tum, ti-tum, ti-tum' etc.

evaluation

 2

Once you have completed this activity, your teacher may give you a worksheet with some notes with which to compare your findings on Shakespeare's rhythm. Think about the discoveries that you made; ask yourself:

* Are they similar to points on the worksheet?

* Can you see the logic behind the name for each unit of rhythm in the notes?

* Will you have to revise some of your ideas?

Resources 1

If you would like to know more about metre in Shakespeare, here are a few suggestions for websites and books that are worth looking at.

Scansion Guide
http://www.holycross.edu/departments/theatre/projects/isp/measure/teachguide/scansion.html

The Poetry Corner
http://www.arches.uga.edu/~narcisse/webwrite/project/scandef.htm#RHYME%20ROYAL

Metre and Scansion (Balliol College, University of Oxford)
http://web.balliol.ox.ac.uk/01/tutors/english/metre.htm

evaluation

3 Review what you have learned using the following points:

★ Can you explain Shakespeare's metre in your own terms?

★ Are there any points that you need to clarify with other students or a teacher?

★ Is there anything you need to do further research on?

E *What effect is produced by Shakespeare's language?*

1–2 hours

comprehension

1 Briefly summarise what is being said in the extracts from *Romeo and Juliet* (pages 31–33).

2 Explain why each character speaks in that particular style of language.

3 What is the average number of syllables in the blank verse in the extracts?

4 What is the name of the metre used by Shakespeare?

5 What are the characteristics of blank verse?

6 How does blank verse differ from rhyming couplets?

analysis

7 Look more closely at the imagery (metaphors or similes) used by Benvolio and continued by Romeo. How does Romeo develop light/dark and black/white imagery in his comparison of Juliet with other young women at the feast?

8 How does Romeo's imagery reveal his feelings towards Juliet?

application

9 Experiment by rewriting either a blank verse passage or Romeo's poetic speech in prose. Evaluate the result of your translation in a paragraph or so. Consider what is lost or gained by changing the form of the speech.

evaluation

10 Discuss, compare and check your answers with a partner. Be prepared to offer some of your answers in a whole-class discussion.

3
hours

knowledge

  1

Read through *one* of these selections from plays by Shakespeare. The one you choose may depend on the texts that are available in your school.

★ *Macbeth*, Act 1, scenes 1–3

★ *A Midsummer Night's Dream*, Act 1

★ *The Merchant of Venice*, Act 1, scenes 1–2

★ *Romeo and Juliet*, Act 1, scenes 1–2.

application

  2

Prepare a role-play for one or two scenes from one of these plays.

? Help

✷ Your performance could be given on an open evening or for a class studying the play.

✷ Your performance could also be taped or filmed; this will help you to evaluate your work on this assignment later.

In your role-play try to:

✷ be conscious of different styles of language

✷ help the audience understand the language and imagery through gestures and movement

✷ think about where you should move and stand and how you should make eye contact with other actors

✷ emphasise any variations in rhythm, for example trochees and spondees, to clarify your character's feeling or meaning.

! Information

By the early 1600s the acting style followed by many actors was 'personation'. The audience expected elaborate language as they were used to poetry. They were also very good listeners, but they might not have been able to follow some of the more difficult speeches. The actors helped them follow speeches and events through exaggerated gestures, movement and speech on the stage.

An interesting comparison can be made with the style of acting used in the era of silent movies. Actors relied on gesture and movement to help audiences understand what they could not hear.

Constance Collier as Lady Macbeth and Sir Herbert Beerbohm Tree as Macbeth in the 1916 film version of *Macbeth* directed by John Emerson.

evaluation

 3

Review your classmates' performances. If you are going to watch videos or listen to taped performances then you may need a whole lesson. The questions for discussion could include the following:

★ What was done well?

★ What could have been done better?

★ What did each individual think of his or her performance?

★ Did anyone discover anything new?

 G *Learning review* **45 minutes**

evaluation

  1

Produce a detailed spidergram or write a report on how Shakespeare uses language. Use all your notes and draw on the things you have learned in this unit to help you:

★ identify Shakespeare's three styles of language

* explain why each style of language is used

* analyse a brief section of Shakespeare's verse

* offer an explanation of why style of language is important for Shakespeare.

Include in your spidergram or report any further questions that you have raised about Shakespeare's language or any ideas that you would like to explore further.

 2 Keep your completed spidergram or report along with other written work in a portfolio, as this will form part of your evidence for completing this assignment.

evaluation

 3 Display your spidergrams and reports so everyone can read, view, discuss and compare them.

4 Discuss what you have learned from working on this assignment. Raise any points or issues that you would like to explore further.

How confident are you that you have achieved the aims of this assignment?

Aim achieved	Not very confident	Reasonably confident	Confident	Very confident
I am able to identify Shakespeare's three styles of language.				
I understand why Shakespeare selected each style of language.				
I can appreciate and analyse blank verse and rhymed couplets.				

Next steps

What is the next step you need to take in order to further your understanding of Shakespeare's texts?

* Try reading the whole of *Romeo and Juliet* on your own. Remember that you can support your reading by watching one or more film versions of the play.

Transformation in Pygmalion

Target

This challenge will enable you to:

★ explore how the transformation theme in *Pygmalion* is linked with the tale of Cinderella

★ consider the role of speech and its association with class

★ explore the strong contextual issue of women's rights

★ consider how Eliza Doolittle and Professor Higgins can or cannot change.

About this assignment

This assignment links to other subjects in the curriculum. Your work may incorporate:

★ drama   ★ history

★ ICT (for Internet research)   ★ media

★ music

Learning styles

For each activity, consider how you might work in the learning style that suits you best:

★ auditory   ★ kinaesthetic   ★ visual   ★ any combination of these.

 A *Research the Cinderella story* **1 hour**

knowledge

 1

Research the Cinderella theme and its history in literature and folktales from around the world. Choose a few tales at random and read them. Make notes as you read to help you with the task below. (You could make linear notes with bullets and headings or a spidergram.)

What elements of the story are the same in all the versions? List between five and ten of these elements. For instance, you could say that Cinderella is usually either abandoned or neglected by her father.

Your school and local libraries will also be useful sources for information. You could also try the websites and books in Resources box 1.

Resources 1

This site is an excellent source of ideas.

http://www.surlalunefairytales.com/cinderella/index.html

For various versions of Cinderella retold over several centuries try The University of Southern Mississippi's *The Cinderella Project*. When you find the site, scroll down and click the link called *archive inventory*:

http://www-dept.usm.edu/~engdept/cinderella/cinderella.html

synthesis

 2

Take 5 minutes to compare your list with a partner's and add to your list any important elements that you did not have before.

evaluation

 3

Spend 10 to 15 minutes discussing your lists and what you have discovered in a whole-class session. Follow up any ideas that seem unusual and agree as a class the main elements of the Cinderella theme. Add any new and interesting points to your notes.

B *Read* Pygmalion

 3–5 hours

Pygmalion (1938).

George Bernard Shaw's play *Pygmalion* is in the same genre as Cinderella.

My Fair Lady (1964).

There are two film versions. The earliest was called *Pygmalion* (1938) and starred Leslie Howard and Wendy Hiller; the more famous version, *My Fair Lady* (1964), starred Rex Harrison and Audrey Hepburn and was adapted from the popular stage musical of the same name. There is usually a stage production of *My Fair Lady* somewhere in the UK. A recent one by Trevor Nunn was very innovative in its interpretation of the play and in the set design.

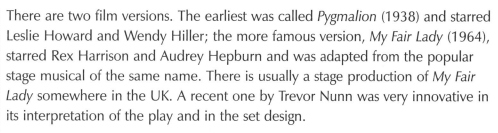

Resources 2

This site has a full copy of Shaw's play.

http://eserver.org/drama/pygmalion/default.html

This site lists performances and other features including a forum for fans to list their comments and queries on the musical.

http://www.myfairladythemusical.com/

This official website for the 1964 film is full of interesting images, videos and audio files that can help you get a feel for the musical if you have not already seen it.

http://www.foxhome.com/myfairlady/index_frames.html

knowledge

 1

Watch at least one of the films or, if possible, see a stage production. This will give an overview of the play before you read it. You should be aware, however, that there are a few differences between the film and the stage versions.

If you manage to see both film versions, or a stage and a film version, write a few notes on how they differ from each other and what you think is gained or lost through any differences in characters, settings or events.

knowledge

 2

Get into a small group that will take responsibility for reading an act or several scenes from the play. Your teacher will ensure that the play is divided up equally between the groups.

In your small group, spend about an hour practising your portion of the text before you read and act it for the class. Remember to use your preferred learning style. Kinaesthetic learners may prefer to move around as they read their lines and act them out.

3

As a class, read the play *Pygmalion*, with each small group performing in turn the scenes they have prepared.

comprehension

 4

After you have read the play, think again about the differences between Shaw's play and the film versions. Leaf through the text to remind yourself of the characters and the scenes. Then consider the following questions, making notes (linear or spidergram) of your answers and findings.

★ Which version do you think works best and why?

★ How does Shaw's play compare with the various versions of Cinderella?

★ What else did you find interesting about the play?

★ Make a list of other texts or films you think have a similar theme.

★ Could the play be compared with Mary Shelley's *Frankenstein*? See the website in Resources box 3 if you would like to investigate this connection further.

 ★ Find out about the mythical king of Cyprus, Pygmalion, and Galatea, the perfect woman that he tried to create. Your teacher will give you a worksheet to help you research the link with the Cypriot king, using Book 10 from Ovid's *Metamorphoses* (written around AD 8).

Resources 3

A useful site for investigating Mary Shelley's *Frankenstein*:

http://www.nlm.nih.gov/hmd/frankenstein/frankhome.html

 C *Speech in* Pygmalion

 2–3 hours

knowledge

 1

Read this scene from near the beginning of Act 2 several times and then work through the questions that follow.

> In Act 2, Eliza Doolittle has dressed up in her finest clothes to see
> Professor Higgins in his house at Wimpole Street. She wants to learn
> how to speak 'more genteel' like 'a lady in a flower shop stead of selling

at the corner of Tottenham Court Rd'. **What motivated her to come was Higgins' boast the previous night, that he could transform her speech to the point where he could 'pass her off as a duchess!'**

MRS PEARCE	*[hesitating, evidently perplexed]* A young woman asks to see you, sir.
HIGGINS	A young woman! What does she want?
MRS PEARCE	Well, sir, she says youll be glad to see her when you know what she's come about. Shes quite a common girl, sir. Very common indeed. I should have sent her away, only I thought perhaps you wanted her to talk into your machines. I hope Ive not done wrong; but really you see such queer people sometimes—youll excuse me, I'm sure, sir—
HIGGINS	Oh, thats all right, Mrs Pearce. Has she an interesting accent?
MRS PEARCE	Oh, something dreadful, sir, really. I dont know how you can take an interest in it.
HIGGINS	*[to Pickering]* Lets have her up. Shew her up, Mrs Pearce *[he rushes across to his working table and picks out a cylinder to use on the phonograph]*.
MRS PEARCE	*[only half resigned to it]* Very well, sir. It's for you to say. *[She goes downstairs].*
HIGGINS	This is rather a bit of luck. I'll shew you how I make records. We'll set her talking; and I'll take it down first in Bell's visible Speech; then in broad Romic; and then we'll get her on the phonograph so that you can turn her on as often as you like with the written transcript before you.
MRS PEARCE	*[returning]* This is the young woman, sir.
	The flower girl enters in state. She has a hat with three ostrich feathers, orange, sky-blue, and red. She has a nearly clean apron, and the shoddy coat has been tidied a little. The pathos of this deplorable figure, with its innocent vanity and consequential air, touches Pickering, who has already straightened himself in the presence of

Mrs Pearce. But as to Higgins, the only distinction he makes between men and women is that when he is neither bullying nor exclaiming to the heavens against some feather-weight cross, he coaxes women as a child coaxes its nurse when it wants to get anything out of her.

HIGGINS   *[brusquely, recognising her with unconcealed disappointment, and at once, babylike, making an intolerable grievance of it]* Why, this is the girl I jotted down last night. Shes no use: Ive got all the records I want of the Lisson Grove lingo; and I'm not going to waste another cylinder on it. *[To the girl]* Be off with you: I dont want you.

THE FLOWER GIRL   Dont you be so saucy. You aint heard what I come for yet. *[To Mrs Pearce, who is waiting at the door for further instructions]* Did you tell him I come in a taxi?

MRS PEARCE   Nonsense, girl! what do you think a gentleman like Mr Higgins cares what you came in?

THE FLOWER GIRL   Oh, we are proud! He aint above giving lessons, not him: I heard him say so. Well, I aint come here to ask for any compliment; and if my money's not good enough I can go elsewhere.

HIGGINS   Good enough for what?

THE FLOWER GIRL   Good enough for ye-oo. Now you know, dont you? I'm come to have lessons, I am. And to pay for em te-oo: make no mistake.

HIGGINS   *[stupent]* W e l l ! ! ! ! *[Recovering his breath with a gasp]* What do you expect me to say to you?

THE FLOWER GIRL   Well, if you was a gentleman, you might ask me to sit down, I think. Dont I tell you I'm bringing you business?

HIGGINS   Pickering: shall we ask this baggage to sit down or shall we throw her out of the window?

THE FLOWER GIRL   *[running away in terror to the piano, where she turns at bay]* Ah-ah-oh-ow-ow-ow-oo! *[Wounded and whimpering]* I wont be called a baggage when Ive offered to pay like any lady.

Motionless, the two men stare at her from the other side of the room, amazed.

PICKERING	*[gently]* What is it you want, my girl?
THE FLOWER GIRL	I want to be a lady in a flower shop stead of selling at the corner of Tottenham Court Road. But they wont take me unless I can talk more genteel. He said he could teach me. Well, here I am ready to pay him—not asking any favor—and he treats me zif I was dirt.
MRS PEARCE	How can you be such a foolish ignorant girl as to think you could afford to pay Mr. Higgins?
THE FLOWER GIRL	Why shouldnt I? I know what lessons cost as well as you do; and I'm ready to pay.
HIGGINS	How much?
THE FLOWER GIRL	*[coming back to him, triumphant]* Now youre talking! I thought youd come off it when you saw a chance of getting back a bit of what you chucked at me last night. *[Confidentially]* Youd had a drop in, hadnt you?
HIGGINS	*[peremptorily]* Sit down.
THE FLOWER GIRL	Oh, if youre going to make a compliment of it–
HIGGINS	[thundering at her] Sit down.
MRS PEARCE	*[severely]* Sit down, girl. Do as youre told.
THE FLOWER GIRL	Ah-ah-ah-ow-ow-oo! *[She stands, half rebellious, half bewildered]*.
PICKERING	*[very courteous]* Wont you sit down? *[He places the stray chair near the hearthrug between himself and Higgins]*.
LIZA	*[coyly]* Dont mind if I do. *[She sits down. Pickering returns to the hearthrug]*.
HIGGINS	Whats your name?
THE FLOWER GIRL	Liza Doolittle.

An extract from *Pygmalion*, Act 2, scene 1

Here are some questions to help you analyse the scene.

Text level

★ Sum up, in one or two paragraphs, what is going on in this extract. Give the extract a context by saying briefly what has happened to bring this scene about.

Sentence level

★ Examine some of the issues that are raised in the extract. Talk with a partner about the points below and make brief notes (linear or spidergram) on what you agree. Where possible, try to give brief quotations to support your ideas. Remember to draw information from Shaw's stage directions too. What can you say about:

  ★ class, and what this implies about society at the time of the play (around 1912)

  ★ each character's use of speech, accent and dialect and the contrasts between them

  ★ what causes characters to be either articulate or inarticulate and why

  ★ the various methods of recording speech

  ★ how different characters treat Eliza and why

  ★ male–female relationships

  ★ how the transformation theme is represented in this extract

  ★ any other issues that you think are important?

Word level

★ Look at Shaw's own spelling and punctuation. How successful is it? What does this imply for our use of punctuation and spelling? What type of punctuation does he prefer?

★ The cockney dialect has changed since Shaw wrote his play. Choose a few of Eliza's lines and update them to modern cockney. Or if you live in an area with another dialect, you could use that. Try reading your translation aloud. Listen carefully to how it sounds.

★ At this point in the play, Eliza does not understand the difference between her own dialect and standard English. What issues does this raise for Eliza? What attitudes do people have towards local dialects today?

3 Get into a small group and compare your answers to the questions in the previous activity. If necessary, amend your notes in the light of new information or a deeper understanding of the questions.

evaluation

4 Appoint a spokesperson for your group and feed back your ideas on questions selected for a whole-class discussion.

D ***Examine the historical context of the play***

1–2 hours

Now you are going to consider how the extract you read in the previous activity relates to the position of women at the time Shaw wrote his play.

knowledge

1 First find out about the type of woman known in the early part of the 20th century as 'the New Woman'. Use the library and the sites in Resources box 4 to help you research and make notes on these questions:

★ Who was 'the New Woman' and what were her aspirations?

★ What was the attitude of most men towards women at that time? What was their view of 'the New Woman'?

analysis

2 Then consider how Eliza compares with 'the New Woman'.

Resources 4

The History of Women's Suffrage

http://www2.worldbook.com/features/whm/html/whm010.html

The New Woman

http://www.history.ohio-state.edu/projects/clash/NewWoman/newwomen-page1.htm

3 Spend 10 to 15 minutes going over your answers with your partner, filling in more details and making connections to the extract where you can.

4 As a class, discuss your answers to the questions above. Then in the light of your contextual understanding of women in the play, look again at the extract on pages 45 to 47. Discuss the two male characters and their reactions to Eliza. What is the outlook for each of them? What kinds of men do they represent? What changes must one or the other make in their attitude towards women?

E *Beyond the script*

3–4 hours

1 Remind yourself of the final exchanges between Professor Higgins and Eliza by reading the last scene of the play, set in Mrs Higgins' house.

2 Write an extra scene for the play. It is probably easiest to add a scene to follow the final act – perhaps a week, or six weeks, or six months after Eliza leaves Higgins. But you can write one to insert at any point in the play that you wish.

Decide your aims in writing the scene before you start, for example you could:

★ aim to further the audience's understanding of the relationship between Eliza and Professor Higgins

★ develop how each character feels about the other by showing any changes or conflicts in their characters

★ show how aspects of 'the new woman' are developing in Eliza's character

★ show how Eliza and Higgins relate to other characters from the play.

If you wish, you could write your scene for the musical version and include a song. You could write both the lyrics and the music or set new lyrics to an existing tune.

Information

In the closing scenes in *My Fair Lady*, Professor Higgins experiences inner conflict in his relationship with Eliza. He admits that he wants Eliza back because he will miss her, but he remains selfish in how he wants to treat her: 'I don't and won't trade in affection.' Eliza wants kindness, and both of them are conscious of her new independence.

In the play, Shaw ensures that they part; in the film and stage musical, however, they are brought together and there is the possibility of a happy ending. But even here, the issue of how Higgins will treat Eliza is left unresolved.

Near the end of the play, Higgins seems only to be thinking of himself as he asks Eliza to order him several luxury items ranging from Stilton cheese to 'reindeer gloves'. Shaw's stage directions reveal that Higgins cannot change in his attitude towards Eliza: 'His cheerful, careless, vigorous voice shews that he is incorrigible.'

In a postscript Shaw argued that 'the rest of the story need not be shown in action' because he thought a happy ending would have been a clichéd and unrealistic ending for his play. The musical and movie of *My Fair Lady* offered audiences the *possibility* of a happy ending, but audiences would have to use their imaginations to decide how the Eliza–Higgins relationship turned out. What would you imagine happens after the end of the play?

 3 Perform your scene to an audience of classmates and teachers, or another class, or an assembly or parents' evening. If you can make an audio or video recording of your performance, this will help you to make an objective evaluation of your work.

evaluation

 4 Hold a brief question and answer session after each performance so that you can explain your ideas and interpretation to your classmates. Your classmates in turn can feed back on what you did well and what you could have done better.

Add any relevant new insights that emerge out of your performances and discussions to the notes that you have already made on Shaw's play.

evaluation

1 Review your learning in this assignment and think about how successful you have been. What did you do well and what could you have done better? Write a few notes on how things turned out, then fill in the assessment grid.

Aim achieved	Not very confident	Reasonably confident	Confident	Very confident
I discovered how the transformation theme is conveyed in Shaw's *Pygmalion*.				
I know how the play links with the tale of Cinderella.				
I considered the role of speech in the play and its association with class.				
I understand the contextual issue of women's rights.				
I considered how Eliza and Higgins could or could not change.				

Next steps

Are there any ideas in connection with the transformation theme that you would like to follow up? One possibility you might like to explore is the more recent play *Educating Rita*, but your research on this or on other assignments may have thrown up other texts or themes that you could compare with Shaw's *Pygmalion*.

Target

This challenge will enable you to:

★ understand that the education of the heart as well as the mind is an important theme in *Great Expectations*

★ see how other themes such as personal growth or lack of growth, wealth and its effects upon the individual, class, and Pip's learning to become a gentleman are related to the theme of education

★ learn what education was like for the majority of the population in Victorian times and to discover Charles Dickens' views on this topic

★ know how the form and style of Dickens' novel was shaped by the expectations of the readership of *All Year Round*, the weekly magazine that serialised *Great Expectations*, publishing the final episode in 1861

★ appreciate Dickens' style as a writer by adapting a chapter from *Great Expectations* for television or for the big screen.

About this assignment

This assignment links to other subjects in the curriculum. Your work may incorporate:

★ drama

★ history

★ media

★ geography

★ ICT (for Internet research)

★ music

Learning styles

For each activity, consider how you might work in the learning style that suits you best:

★ auditory   ★ kinaesthetic   ★ visual   ★ any combination of these.

A *What was it like to be a child in Victorian times?*

 1–2 hours

knowledge

1 Find out what education and children's lives were like at the time when Charles Dickens wrote his novels. Write some brief notes that you can refer to later during a class discussion on this topic.

Help

Visual-linguistic learners could arrange their notes by creating topic headings and then writing notes as bullet points under those headings.

Visual-spatial learners could arrange their notes in chart form or as a spidergram.

Whatever your preferred learning style, you could convert your notes into a thinking brace map, like the one below, to help you organise and prioritise your ideas. You could add more levels according to the information you discover in the course of your research.

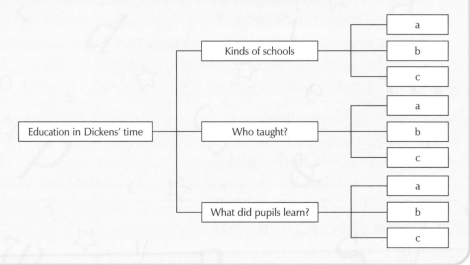

Resources 1

These websites and the books beneath will have all the information that you need to help you write your notes.

Pip's World: a hypertext on Charles Dickens' *Great Expectations*
http://www.umd.umich.edu/casl/hum/eng/classes/434/geweb/TITLESPA.htm

So What Was It Like For Victorian Children?
http://www.richard-york.co.uk/past/vicchildren.html

Victorian People
http://www.richard-york.co.uk/past/vicpeople1.html

Victorian London Street Life in Historic Photographs
by John Thompson, Dover Publications (1994)

Victorian London Revealed: Gustav Doré's Metropolis,
Penguin Books (2001)

synthesis

  2

Spend about 20 minutes comparing and arranging the information that you have discovered in order to get ready for a class discussion.

evaluation

  3

Discuss your findings as a class and make a note of any interesting discoveries or information that you think will help you with this assignment. Make a note also of any parts of the topic where you think that you may need to carry out further research.

B Find out in the next instalment…

1–2 hours

knowledge

  1

Spend about an hour researching the background to *Great Expectations*. Find out how Dickens went about writing the novel in the form of a serial. Can you see any features that the Victorian serialised novels had in common with modern soap operas such as *EastEnders* and *Coronation Street*?

The books and websites in Resources box 2 will help you with this research and also with tasks later on in this assignment. So before you start, scan the tasks coming later and make a note of what you should look out for. Then gather information that you think might be interesting or relevant as you go along. You could print off any pictures and notes that look useful. But be selective – do not print everything!

Resources 2

The following websites will be helpful for tasks throughout this assignment.

The best site for Dickens and *Great Expectations* is

David Perdue's Charles Dickens Page
http://www.fidnet.com/~dap1955/dickens/index.html
http://www.fidnet.com/~dap1955/dickens/expectations.html

See David's map at:

http://www.fidnet.com/~dap1955/dickens/dickens_london_map.html

Other sites recommended for this task include:

Charles Dickens, *Great Expectations* Index
**http://www.vanderbilt.edu/AnS/english/English104W-15/
greatexpectations[index].htm**

synthesis

2 Gather your resources and notes and spend 20 minutes or so comparing what you have found out before you have a general discussion about your research in class.

evaluation

3 Discuss your findings as a class. Make a note of any interesting discoveries made by other students including the details of any resources (e.g. book titles or website addresses) you would like to follow up.

C *How does Dickens convey his ideas?*   2–3 hours

comprehension

1 Read this abridged extract from Chapter 7 of *Great Expectations* straight through, then look at the two questions below. Read the text a second time keeping these general questions in mind. Your teacher may give you a copy of the text that you can annotate.

★ What was Dickens' view of the kind of education available to the mass of the people and what he would like to see changed?

★ How does this extract foreshadow what Pip comes to understand towards the end of the novel: that the education of the heart is as important as the education of the mind. In the second half of the novel, Pip's unearned wealth and the other trappings of being 'a gentleman' cause him to be ashamed of simple men like his brother-in-law and the blacksmith, Joe Gargery. In this extract Pip receives an early lesson, that he then forgets for a time: that goodness and forgiveness can be learned.

Mr Wopsle's great-aunt kept an evening school in the village; that is to say, she was a ridiculous old woman of limited means and unlimited infirmity, who used to go to sleep from six to seven every evening, in the society of youth who paid twopence per week each, for the improving opportunity of seeing her do it. She rented a small cottage, and Mr Wopsle had the room upstairs, where we students used to overhear him reading aloud in a most dignified and terrific manner, and occasionally bumping on the ceiling. There was a fiction that Mr Wopsle 'examined' the scholars, once a quarter. What he did on those occasions was to turn up his cuffs, stick up his hair, and give us Mark Antony's oration over the body of Caesar […]

Mr Wopsle's great-aunt, besides keeping this Educational Institution, kept in the same room – a little general shop. She had no idea what stock she had, or what the price of anything in it was; but there was a little greasy memorandum-book kept in a drawer, which served as a Catalogue of Prices, and by this oracle Biddy arranged all the shop transactions. Biddy was Mr Wopsle's great-aunt's grand-daughter; I confess myself quiet unequal to the working out of the problem, what relation she was to Mr Wopsle. She was an orphan like myself; like me, too, had been brought up by hand […]

Much of my unassisted self, and more by the help of Biddy than of Mr Wopsle's great-aunt, I struggled through the alphabet as if it had been a bramble-bush; getting considerably worried and scratched by every letter. After that, I fell among those thieves, the nine figures, who seemed every evening to do something new to disguise themselves and baffle recognition. But, at last I began, in a purblind groping way, to read, write, and cipher, on the very smallest scale.

One night, I was writing in the chimney-corner with my slate, expending great efforts on the production of a letter to Joe. I think it must have been a full year after our hunt upon the marshes, for it was a long time after, and it was winter, and a hard frost. With an alphabet on the hearth at my feet for reference, I contrived in an hour or two to print and smear this epistle:

'MI DeER JO i opE U r krWitE wEll i opE i
sHAl soN B haBell 4 2 teEDge U JO aN theN
wE sHOrl B sO gLOdd aN wEn i M preNgtD 2 U
JO woT larX AN blEvE ME inF xn PiP.'

There was no indispensable necessity for my communicating with Joe by letter, inasmuch as he sat beside me and we were alone. But, I delivered this written communication (slate and all) with my own hand, and Joe received it as a miracle of erudition.

'I say, Pip, old chap!' cried Joe, opening his blue eyes wide, 'what a scholar you are! Ain't you?'

'I should like to be,' said I, glancing at the slate as he held it: with a misgiving that the writing was rather hilly.

'Why, here's a J,' said Joe, 'and a O equal to anythink! Here's a J and a O, Pip, and a J-O, Joe.'

Young Pip (Anthony Wager) and Joe Gargery (Bernard Miles) in the 1946 film version of *Great Expectations* directed by David Lean.

I had never heard Joe read aloud to any greater extent than this monosyllable, and I had observed at church last Sunday, when I accidentally held our Prayer-book upside down, that it seemed to suit his convenience quite as well as if it had been all right. Wishing to embrace the present occasion of finding out whether in teaching Joe, I should have to begin quite at the beginning, I said, Ah! But read the rest, Jo.'

'The rest, eh, Pip?' said Joe, looking at it with a slowly searching eye, 'One, two, three. Why, here's three Js, and three Os, and three J-O, Joes in it, Pip!'

I leaned over Joe, and, with the aid of my forefinger, read him the whole letter.

'Astonishing!' said Joe, when I had finished. 'You ARE a scholar.'

'How do you spell Gargery, Joe?' I asked him, with a modest patronage.

'I don't spell it at all,' said Joe.

'But supposing you did?'

'It can't be supposed,' said Joe. 'Tho' I'm oncommon fond of reading, too.'

'Are you, Joe?'

'On-common. Give me,' said Joe, 'a good book, or a good newspaper, and sit me down afore a good fire, and I ask no better. Lord!' he continued, after rubbing his knees a little, 'when you *do* come to a J and a O, and says you, "Here, at last, is a J-O, Joe," how interesting reading is!'

I derived from this last, that Joe's education, like Steam, was yet in its infancy. Pursuing the subject, I inquired:

'Didn't you ever go to school, Joe, when you were as little as me?'

'No, Pip.'

'Why didn't you ever go to school, Joe, when you were as little as me?'

'Well, Pip,' said Joe, taking up the poker, and settling himself to his usual occupation when he was thoughtful, of slowly raking the fire between the lower bars: 'I'll tell you. My father, Pip, he were given to drink, and when he were overtook with drink, he hammered away at my mother, most onmerciful. It were a'most the only hammering he did, indeed, 'xcepting at myself. And he hammered at me with a wigour only to be equalled by the wigour with which he didn't hammer at his anvil. – You're a-listening and understanding, Pip?'

'Yes, Joe.'

''Consequence, my mother and me we ran away from my father, several times; and then my mother she'd go out to work, and she'd say, "Joe," she'd say, "now, please God, you shall have some schooling, child," and she'd put me to school. But my father were that good in his hart that he couldn't abear to be without us. So, he'd come with a most tremenjous crowd and make such a row at the doors of the houses where we was, that they used to be obligated to have no more to do with us and to give us up to him. And then he took us home and hammered us. Which, you see, Pip,' said Joe, pausing in his meditative raking of the fire, and looking at me, 'were a drawback on my learning.'

'Certainly, poor Joe!'

'Though mind you, Pip,' said Joe, with a judicial touch or two of the poker on the top bar, 'rendering unto all their doo, and maintaining equal justice betwixt man and man, my father were that good in his hart, don't you see?'

'I present Joe to Miss Havisham', an illustration by S. W. Pailthorp from the 1885 edition of *Great Expectations*.

I didn't see; but I didn't say so.

'Well!' Joe pursued, 'somebody must keep the pot a-biling, Pip, or the pot won't bile, don't you know?'

I saw that, and said so.

'Consequence, my father didn't make objections to my going to work; so I went to work at my present calling, which were his too, if he would have followed it, and I worked tolerable hard, I assure *you*, Pip. In time I were able to keep him, and I kept him till he went off in a purple leptic fit. And it were my intentions to have had put upon his tombstone that Whatsume'er the failings on his part, Remember reader he were that good in his hart.'

Joe recited this couplet with such manifest pride and careful perspicuity, that I asked him if he had made it himself.

'I made it,' said Joe, 'my own self. I made it in a moment. It was like striking out a horseshoe complete, in a single blow. I never was so much surprised in all my life – couldn't credit my own ed – to tell you the truth, hardly believed it *were* my own ed. As I was saying, Pip, it were my intentions to have had it cut over him; but poetry costs money, cut it how you will, small or large, and it were not done. Not to mention bearers, all the money that could be spared were wanted for my mother. She were in poor elth, and quite broke. She waren't long of following, poor soul, and her share of peace come round at last.'

Joe's blue eyes turned a little watery; he rubbed, first one of them, and then the other, in a most uncongenial and uncomfortable manner, with the round knob on the top of the poker.

'It were but lonesome then,' said Joe, 'living here alone, and I got acquainted with your sister. Now, Pip'; Joe looked firmly at me, as if he knew I was not going to agree with him; 'your sister is a fine figure of a woman.'

I could not help looking at the fire, in an obvious state of doubt.

'Whatever family opinions, or whatever the world's opinions, on that subject may be, Pip, your sister is,' Joe tapped the top bar with the poker after every word following, 'a – fine – figure – of – a – woman!'

I could think of nothing better to say than 'I am glad you think so, Joe.'

'So am I,' returned Joe, catching me up. 'I am glad I think so, Pip. A little redness or a little matter of Bone, here or there, what does it signify to Me?'

I sagaciously observed, if it didn't signify to him, to whom did it signify?

'Certainly!' assented Joe. 'That's it. You're right, old chap! When I got acquainted with your sister, it were the talk how she was bringing you up by hand. Very kind of her too, all the folks said, and I said, along with all the folks. As to you,' Joe pursued with a countenance expressive of seeing something very nasty indeed: 'if you could have been aware how small and flabby and mean you was, dear me, you'd have formed the most contemptible opinions of yourself!'

Not exactly relishing this, I said, 'Never mind me, Joe.'

'But I did mind you, Pip,' he returned with tender simplicity. 'When I offered to your sister to keep company, and to be asked in church at such times as she was willing and ready to come to the forge, I said to her, "And bring the poor little child. God bless the poor little child," I said to your sister, "there's room for *him* at the forge!"'

I broke out crying and begging pardon, and hugged Joe round the neck: who dropped the poker to hug me, and to say, 'Ever the best of friends; ain't us, Pip? Don't cry, old chap!'

When this little interruption was over, Joe resumed:

'Well, you see, Pip, and here we are! That's about where it lights; here we are! Now, when you take me in hand in my learning, Pip (and I tell you beforehand I am awful dull, most awful dull), Mrs Joe mustn't see too much of what we're up to. It must be done, as I may say, on the sly. And why on the sly? I'll tell you why, Pip.'

He had taken up the poker again; without which, I doubt if he could have proceeded in his demonstration.

'Your sister is given to government.'

'Given to government, Joe?' I was startled, for I had some shadowy idea (and I am afraid I must add, hope) that Joe had divorced her in a favour of the Lords of the Admiralty, or Treasury.

'Given to government,' said Joe. 'Which I meantersay the government of you and myself.'

'Oh!'

'And she an't over partial to having scholars on the premises,' Joe continued, 'and in partickler would not be over partial to my being a scholar, for fear as I might rise. Like a sort of rebel, don't you see?'

I was going to retort with an inquiry, and had got as far as 'Why—' when Joe stopped me.

'Stay a bit. I know what you're a-going to say, Pip; stay a bit! I don't deny that your sister comes the Mo-gul over us, now and again. I don't deny that she do throw us back-falls, and that she do drop down upon us heavy. At such times as when your sister is on the Ram-page, Pip,' Joe sank his voice to a whisper and glanced at the door, 'candour compels fur to admit that she is a Buster.'

Joe pronounced this word, as if it began with at least twelve capital Bs.

'Why don't I rise? That were your observation when I broke it off, Pip?'

'Yes, Joe.'

'Well,' said Joe, passing the poker into his left hand, that he might feel his whisker; and I had no hope of him whenever he took to that placid occupation; 'your sister's a master-mind. A master-mind.'

'What's that?' I asked, in some hope of bringing him to a stand. But, Joe was readier with his definition than I had expected, and completely stopped me by arguing circularly, and answering with a fixed look, 'Her.'

'And I ain't a master-mind,' Joe resumed, when he had unfixed his look, and got back to his whisker. 'And last of all, Pip – and this I want to say very serious to you, old chap – I see so much in my poor mother, of a woman drudging and slaving and breaking her honest hart and never getting no peace in her mortal days, that I'm dead afeerd of going wrong in the way of not doing what's right by a woman, and I'd fur rather of the two go wrong the t'other way, and be a little ill-conwenienced myself. I wish it was only me that got put out, Pip; I wish there warn't no Tickler for you, old chap; I wish I could take it all on myself; but this is the up-and-down-and-straight on it, Pip, and I hope you'll overlook shortcomings.'

Young as I was, I believe that I dated a new admiration of Joe from that night. We were equals afterwards, as we had been before; but, afterwards at quiet times when I sat looking at Joe and thinking about him, I had a new sensation of feeling conscious that I was looking up to Joe in my heart.

Extract from *Great Expectations*, Chapter 7

Here are some questions to help you continue your study of this extract. You do not have to answer every question, but make sure that your research includes some work at each level. Use Resources box 2 and Resources box 3 to help you. Make notes in a way that suits your most favoured learning style (see the Help box for some suggestions).

Help

Visual-linguistic learners could use formal notes; auditory learners may prefer to tape record their ideas before writing down their answers; bodily-kinesthetic learners could type up their notes on a computer; visual-spatial learners could produce spidergrams or a character map like the example below:

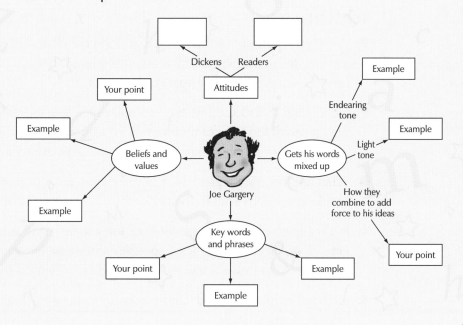

Resources 3

http://www.learn.co.uk/default.asp?WCI=SubUnit&WCU=4308

http://www.learn.co.uk/default.asp?WCI=Unit&WCU=97

Have a look at this site for a fascinating collection of links on English dialects throughout the world. Try out some of the dialect translators.
http://www.courses.fas.harvard.edu/~ling80/wwwlinks/

Text level

★ Sum up in one or two paragraphs the main themes and issues explored in this extract. A theme is a repeated idea or message.

★ Dickens uses a great deal of irony in the novel. (Irony is when a speaker humorously or critically means the opposite of what he or she says.) Characters can be said to be ironic when they say one thing but mean another. Briefly explain how the narrator is ironic about the 'evening school', quoting a couple of words, phrases or sentences to support your points.

★ What is Dickens implying about the state and provision of education for the wider population of England?

★ What kind of writing seems to dominate in this extract: description or dialogue, or is it equally divided between the two? Give reasons for your answer.

★ How did you feel when you read this extract?

Sentence level

★ Who is the narrator of this extract (and the novel) and at what point in life are they telling the story? Think about the tense that the narrator uses and note a couple of lines to support your point.

★ Identify the dialect used by the two main speakers. How does each character's dialect reveal the level of their formal education? Remember that the narrator is probably revising his original speech as he later gained a formal education.

★ What are the main reasons and purposes for using local dialect or for speaking standard English today?

★ Pip is a keen observer and listener of Joe's speech and actions in this extract. How does Dickens make Joe's speech memorable by what Joe says and what he does? Write down a few examples and comment on them.

★ Victorian readers expected and enjoyed moving and sentimental passages from Dickens. Choose a few lines from this extract that you found moving, or that you think a Victorian audience would have found moving, and explain how they achieved their effect.

★ Select one or two lines where the language seems old fashioned and that show the text was written over 140 years ago.

Word level

★ Select four or five unusual or unfamiliar words or phrases that show that this text was written over 140 years ago. What words or phrases might be used instead in a modern text?

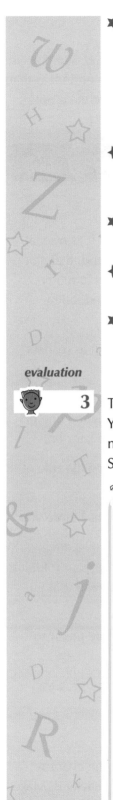

* Dickens was famous for his unusual and original choice of names for his characters. Usually a character's name implied something about their character and indicated whether the readers were intended to take them seriously or not. Choose the names of two or three characters in this extract and consider what could be implied by their names. Go on to explain whether we should consider these characters seriously or not.

* Joe Gargery is a blacksmith with no formal education. Find a few examples of words he either mispronounces or simply gets wrong. What is the effect upon the reader when he does this?

* How does the tone of Joe's mispronounced words ultimately add force to his values and beliefs?

* What do you think is Dickens' attitude towards Joe? What is the reader expected to make of Joe and his ideas? What does Joe symbolise?

* What key words or phrases are associated with Joe? How are these connected to what Joe can teach Pip?

evaluation

 3 Take some time to reflect upon your answers in the form that you made them. You need to monitor and regulate what you have learned by going over your notes and asking yourself questions about what you did and the way you did it. See the Help box for more on this.

Help

Metacognition

Metacognition means 'thinking about thinking'. It is what you do when you check and regulate what you learn and how you learn it. You use similar skills when you plan various kinds of writing and when you think through what you need to learn next. Every successful student uses metacognition, asking questions such as the ones below.

* Do I need to add more details, points or examples to my answers?

* Have I checked my answers for errors?

* Can I defend my answers with relevant evidence from the text?

* Are there any topics and ideas that I need to research further by asking a teacher or by researching on my own?

* What other questions do I need to ask to self-check my understanding and take my learning further?

evaluation

4 Discuss your answers to the text-level, sentence-level and word-level questions in a whole-class discussion. Again, add to your notes any fresh points and ideas that you think help your understanding in this part of the assignment. Make a note also of any points that you need to research further.

D *Read the novel*

12 hours

knowledge

1 Now read the rest of the novel *Great Expectations*. You could read it as a serial, which is how it was first read in the weekly magazine, *All Year Round*, that Dickens also edited. Dickens wrote most of the novel two chapters at a time. Some modern editions, including the edition by Penguin Classics, edited by Angus Calder, mark the end of each serial with a star.

Read the first stage of *Great Expectations* (to the end of Chapter 19) as readers' theatre. Organise this as follows.

★ The class should be divided into small groups, with each group assigned responsibility for two chapters. One group may need to be assigned one or three chapters. If chapters are left over, simply repeat the cycle later on.

★ Each member of the group should take a role. The reader taking the role of Pip is also the narrator.

★ Read through your assigned chapters and practise a few sections before you act out your parts either expressively or dramatically in class.

★ There is no need to make a script from your book or memorise your role. Just mark up your part, familiarise yourself with the character and read it as expressively as you can.

★ As usual, work to your strengths: bodily-kinesthetic learners may prefer to move around as they read their parts.

★ Each group takes it in turn to perform their two chapters as they progress through the first stage.

comprehension

2 After each group's reading spend some time as a class discussing the characters and the themes (messages or ideas) that you have worked on in Activity B. Make a note of any new insights or discoveries that you make.

The time you spend in discussion for each chapter will depend upon the significance of the themes in it. Some discussions will be brief but some may last 20 minutes or more. Take as long as you need to explore your ideas.

You could complete your reading of the novel on your own at home or with readers' theatre if you have the time.

E *Write the screenplay*

2 hours

application

1 One way to get to know Dickens' written style better is to adapt a chapter or a scene from the novel for a modern audience. Think about the most dramatically interesting chapter that you read or that you heard someone else read in class, then consider how you could rewrite it as a scene for television or film. You can work alone, in pairs or in a group. You should also aim to perform and perhaps record your final result. A real audience for your scenes and performances could comprise:

★ your class

★ other classes from the same or other year groups

★ students from another school, secondary or primary

★ parents and guests at an open evening

★ a special assembly

★ your local community.

WS 12

Help

Tips for writing screenplays

If your screenplay is going to appeal to a modern audience you will have to adapt Dickens' prose. Here are a few pointers to help you create your screenplay.

⚹ Have a clear idea of the audience that you expect to reach, for example your peer group.

⚹ Have a clear idea of what you want your audience to understand after seeing your scene. Think about the themes and ideas that you would like to emphasise.

⚹ Edit description by keeping it to the bare minimum. Try to suggest as much as possible through dialogue.

- You may need to introduce dialogue of your own in places to help smooth the progress of your scene or to replace some of Dickens' dialogue.

- Cut down on any repetition of dialogue, unless it is crucial for the dramatic impact that you wish to make.

- Consider each character's personality and motives as you write their lines.

- Consider how props, details of dress and actors' gestures can convey points and ideas.

- Shape your scene by having a clear beginning, middle and end.

- See Resources box 4 for sites giving more advice from the experts.

Resources 4

Several experts share their know-how on writing screenplays at this BBC website! Work your way through the advice by clicking through the tick list on the right-hand side of the page.

http://www.bbc.co.uk/worldservice/arts/features/howtowrite/ screenplay.shtml

Find out how others turned *Great Expectations* into a script. A playscript for readers' theatre that has part of the novel and suggestions for songs to help set the atmosphere can be found at:

http://humwww.ucsc.edu/dickens/DEA/GEresources/ Readers.Theatre.Script.GE.html

evaluation

 2

As each group performs their chosen scenes, be prepared to give plenty of support and encouragement as well as advice. Remember that it is not easy to perform in front of others, so building confidence is important. Point out what can be improved and praise what has been done well.

For a public performance, it may be necessary to perform only a sample of what the class has produced. You could vote for your favourite performances and pull together to produce a performance of those scenes.

3

After you have performed your scenes, watch a film version of the novel and pay particular attention to the adaptation of your scene. Replay the scene several times to examine the changes and choices that were made and consider the reasons why they were made. Scriptwriters and directors often rewrite their scripts many times during the making of a film.

Resources 5

Information about David Lean's classic film adaptation can be found at Teach With Movies:

http://www.teachwithmovies.org/guides/great-expectations.html

E *Learning review*  **30 minutes**

evaluation

 1

Fill in the assessment grid and add it to the notes and work from this assignment that you already have in your portfolio.

 WS 13

How confident are you that you achieved the aims of this challenge?

Aim achieved	Not very confident	Reasonably confident	Confident	Very confident
I understand that education of the heart as well as the mind is a key theme in *Great Expectations*.				
I understand how the novel's other themes link with the theme of education.				

continued overleaf

Aim achieved	Not very confident	Reasonably confident	Confident	Very confident
I discovered what education was like in Victorian times as well as Dickens' views on it.				
I know how the form and style of Dickens' novel was shaped by the expectations of his readership.				
I appreciate Dickens' writing style.				

If any one of your answers is in the first column, go over the relevant parts of the assignment again to review key points and ideas.

evaluation

 2

Consider also *how* you learned during this assignment. Use the checklist below to assess your skills as an independent learner. What were the skills that you developed? What skills do you need to develop further?

A checklist of intrapersonal study skills:

★ I showed good or excellent interpersonal skills when I worked in pairs, or groups or with the whole class.

★ My research skills have improved through my familiarity with the Internet or libraries.

★ I used my favoured learning style effectively during this assignment.

★ I showed creative flair and ability during this assignment.

★ I worked in a flexible way.

★ I was able to integrate new ideas in my work.

★ I showed persistence as I worked steadily towards the main aims of this challenge.

★ I returned to ideas that I did not understand and found new or different answers for them.

* I was able to accept different interpretations and ideas made by other students and can acknowledge diversity.

* I discovered some unusual ideas and information during my research.

* I gained confidence in myself as a learner.

* I showed energy and commitment during this challenge.

* I reflected on what I knew and used metacognition when I needed to.

Write down any other further points that you would like to make about your level of study skills.

If you did not agree with every point on the checklist, briefly state what happened. Then make a note of any study skills targets that you wish to achieve in your next challenge.

Resources 6

Find out more about intrapersonal intelligence and the other intelligences that make up the set of multiple intelligences by visiting this website:

The Gardner School
http://www.gardnerschool.org/multiple_intelligences.html

Next steps

Your next step could be any or all of the following.

* If you have not already done so, complete your reading of *Great Expectations*.

* Read another novel by Dickens or a novel by a contemporary writer. Good choices would be *Jane Eyre* by Charlotte Brontë or *The Moonstone* by Wilkie Collins; you could compare the themes of either of these novels with *Great Expectations*.

* Produce a colourful timeline chart for *Great Expectations* in which you set out the novel's themes and how they relate to the main characters.

The development of the sonnet

Target

This challenge will enable you to:

* find out what sonnets are
* work out how they are constructed
* understand how poets adapted sonnets over time
* write sonnets of your own.

About this assignment

 This assignment links to other subjects in the curriculum. Your work may incorporate:

* drama
* ICT (for Internet research)
* history
* music

Learning styles

For each activity, consider how you might work in the learning style that suits you best:

* auditory
* kinaesthetic
* visual
* any combination of these.

A — What can poetry be about?

 1 hour

knowledge

 1 What do you think is suitable subject matter for poetry? What emotions and experiences are often found in poems? Can they be stories or portraits? Should they have a purpose or a moral? What aspects of human experience do you think poets capture in poems?

Let your imagination wander by producing a bubble diagram on what you think poetry can be about. If you agree with 'love' and 'friendship' you can start with those. Add more bubbles as you need them to link related ideas.

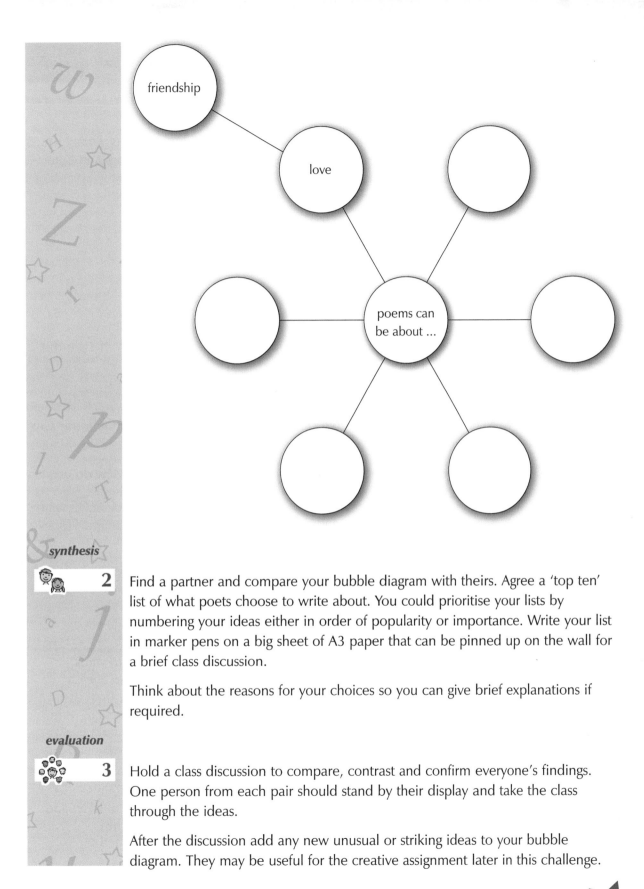

2 Find a partner and compare your bubble diagram with theirs. Agree a 'top ten' list of what poets choose to write about. You could prioritise your lists by numbering your ideas either in order of popularity or importance. Write your list in marker pens on a big sheet of A3 paper that can be pinned up on the wall for a brief class discussion.

Think about the reasons for your choices so you can give brief explanations if required.

evaluation

3 Hold a class discussion to compare, contrast and confirm everyone's findings. One person from each pair should stand by their display and take the class through the ideas.

After the discussion add any new unusual or striking ideas to your bubble diagram. They may be useful for the creative assignment later in this challenge.

knowledge

1 Find out about the form of poem called a sonnet. Use the questions below to help in your research and make notes either in the form of headings and bullet points or bubble diagram.

✴ What is a sonnet and what does it look like?

✴ How did the sonnet get its name and what does the word 'sonnet' literally mean?

✴ Where did sonnets originate?

✴ Who brought them to England and why?

✴ How are sonnets structured? (How do poets construct them?) What are the terms for the different parts of a sonnet?

✴ Why have poets varied the form of their sonnets?

✴ Which poet or poets, in your opinion, are the best adapters of the form? Give reasons for your answer.

✴ What were the main subjects or themes of the early sonnets? Why do you think poets chose these themes?

✴ Give examples of themes and subject matter in later sonnets.

✴ What else can you discover about the sonnet?

Help

Research tips

Go to the school library and ask your librarian to point you towards good reference books. You could always start with the *Oxford English Dictionary*. (If you use the OED, you may need some advice from your librarian or a teacher on how to make best use of it.) Alternatively, or in addition, you could do some research on the Internet. You could use a search engine such as Google to search for material on sonnets or go straight to the websites listed in Resources box 1.

Whatever you do, remember that you only have about an hour, so use your time efficiently. To do this, you will need to skim (read quickly) and scan (pick out the relevant pieces of information) to gather the information that you need. Think about the skills that you need to gather your information efficiently as well as effectively. Keep asking yourself, 'Is the way I am working producing the required results or do I need to change tack and try another method?'

You could also divide up the questions between you and your partner and then pool your discoveries when you return to class for the whole group session.

Resources 1

The amazing website of Shakespeare's Sonnets
http://www.shakespeares-sonnets.com/

Sonnet Central: an archive of English sonnets
http://www.sonnets.org/
(Be sure to scroll down and check out the Early Sonnets of this great website!)

http://web.balliol.ox.ac.uk/01/tutors/english/sonnet-ex.html

synthesis

 2

In small groups, take about 15 minutes to share the information that you each discovered. Agree on the important points and select a speaker to present your points to the class.

evaluation

 3

Share and reflect on what you found out in a whole-class discussion of about 30 minutes. Do not worry at this stage if what you have to say is still quite general. If you can explain the background of sonnets and how they are constructed you will be on track for more detailed work later in this challenge.

Again, during the discussion make notes on any points mentioned that you had not come across before: these may be very useful later on in this assignment.

 C *What makes a sonnet?*   *1–2 hours*

comprehension

 1

Read this sonnet by Shakespeare several times. It may help to read it aloud. Then consider each of the questions below and note your ideas in linear form or as a spidergram.

- Think about how the poem is organised. Count the number of lines, and the number of syllables in each line. Look carefully at the rhymes and notice how they help divide the poem into sections. How does this affect the poem's meaning? (Look at the Information box for help with rhyme schemes and how to apply them.)

- Think about the subject matter. What do you think the sonnet is about? Why and how does Shakespeare evoke the senses?

- Is there anything else about this poem that entitles it to be described as a sonnet? What is the term for the structure of this sonnet?

- What is witty about this poem? What, in your view, is Shakespeare setting out to achieve here?

Remember to use a good dictionary if you need to check the meanings of any words in the poem.

This 1588 portrait miniature by Nicholas Hilliard shows a dashing young man, believed to be Shakespeare, holding the hand of a mystery woman.

My mistress' eyes are nothing like the sun;
Coral is far more red, than her lips' red;
If snow be white, why then her breasts are dun;
If hairs be wires, black wires grow on her head;
I have seen roses damasked, red and white,
But no such roses see I in her cheeks;
And in some perfumes is there more delight
Than in the breath that from my mistress reeks.
I love to hear her speak, yet well I know,
That music hath a far more pleasing sound;
I grant I never saw a goddess go;
My mistress when she walks treads on the ground.
   And yet, by heaven, I think my love as rare
   As any she belied with false compare.

Sonnet 130, William Shakespeare

Information

Rhyme schemes

The rhyme scheme of a poem is *usually* closely linked with the way the verse is structured. It refers to the pattern of rhymes in a stanza or a section of verse and is usually shown by an alphabetical code. Starting with the letter A, each rhyme is given a letter. Every time a new rhyme occurs, it is labelled with the next letter in the alphabet. Look at the example below to see how a young, late 18th-century poet constructed her rhyme scheme.

Caroline Symmons died of consumption (tuberculosis) at age 14; she wrote this moving sonnet around 1800, when she was only 11.

To Her Young Friend

No moon now blushes on the enamoured sight;	A
No genial sun now warms the torpid lay	B
Since February sternly checked his ray	B
When Lucy's eyes first beamed their azure light.	A
What though no vernal flowers my hand invite	A
To crop their fragrance for your natal day;	B
Lucy, for you the snowdrop and the bay	B
Shall blend the unfading green and modest white.	A
Though on your natal day with aspect bleak	C
Stern winter frown, in icy garments dressed,	D
Still may the rosy summer robe your cheek	C
And the green spring still bud within your breast:	D
Till, the world fading on your closing eyes,	E
You find a golden autumn in the skies.	E

Caroline Symmons

You may like to study this poem further. Remember to use a good dictionary to identify any unusual words. Can you name the style of her sonnet?

evaluation

 **2**

Use a whole-class discussion to share your ideas and to fill in any blanks in your knowledge or understanding. Make a note of any interesting or unusual contributions by other students so you can get an even better understanding of the topic.

Are you confident that you are not only able to identify a sonnet but give the characteristics of several types of sonnets?

  1   Read the following three sonnets several times. Their titles and the poets who wrote them have been deliberately omitted.

Text 1

Shall I compare thee to a summer's day?
Thou art more lovely and more temperate:
Rough winds do shake the darling buds of May,
And summer's lease hath all too short a date:
Sometime too hot the eye of heaven shines
And often is his gold complexion dimmed;
And every fair from fair sometime declines;
By chance, or nature's changing course, untrimmed;
But thy eternal summer shall not fade,
Nor lose possession of that fair thou ow'st,
Nor shall death brag thou wander'st in his shade
When in eternal lines to time thou grow'st:
    So long as men can breathe or eyes can see,
    So long lives this, and this gives life to thee.

Text 2

How do I love thee? Let me count the ways.
I love thee to the depth and breadth and height
My soul can reach, when feeling out of sight
For the ends of Being and ideal Grace.
I love thee to the level of every day's
Most quiet need, by sun and candlelight.
I love thee freely, as men strive for Right;
I love thee purely, as they turn from Praise.
I love thee with the passion put to use
In my old griefs, and with my childhood's faith.
I love thee with a love I seemed to lose
With my lost saints, – I love thee with the breath,
Smiles, tears, of all my life! – and, if God choose,
I shall but love thee better after death.

Text 3

A shilling life will give you all the facts:
How father beat him, how he ran away,
What were the struggles of his youth, what acts
Made him the greatest figure of his day;
Of how he fought, fished, hunted, worked all night,
Though giddy, climbed new mountains; named a sea;
Some of the last researchers even write
Love made him weep his pints like you and me.

With all his honours on, he sighed for one
Who, say astonished critics, lived at home;
Did little jobs about the house with skill
And nothing else; could whistle, would sit still
Or potter round the garden; answered some
Of his long marvellous letters but kept none.

analysis

2 Compare the three sonnets, using the questions below to guide you. You do not have to answer every single question, but ensure that you do some at each level.

Produce your notes in the format that suits you best, for example as formal notes or as spidergrams.

Text level

★ Examine the poems' structures. Which type of sonnet is each one?

★ What is similar or different about each poem's main theme or message?

Sentence level

★ Compare the sonnets' styles of language, for example are they archaic, modern, formal, informal, argumentative, reflective, elevated or ironic?

★ Do the sonnets conform to expected patterns or do they break rules?

★ Look at the type of language used in each sonnet and make an educated guess as to when it was written.

Word level

★ Think about how the poet's diction (words and phrases) contributes to each poem's tone. Try to explain any unusual word choices and think about why certain words are more meaningful and appropriate than others. (Poets think very carefully about the selection of every word.)

➤ Do the same with the poems' imagery (metaphors and similes). Identify striking or unusual imagery and explain how it helps realise meaning in the poems.

Evaluation

★ Make up an appropriate title for each sonnet.

★ Choose the sonnet that you liked most and give reasons for your choice.

★ Make a note of anything that intrigued you about the poems and be prepared to raise your points in a whole-class discussion.

Resources 2

If you need to remind yourself of the techniques and terms used in poetry, here is a useful website where you will find a good dictionary of literary terms:

**http://www.lausd.k12.ca.us/lausd/resources/shakespeare/
Literary.Terms.Menu.html**

evaluation

  3

Be prepared to offer contributions in the whole-class feedback session. Write notes on points for which you needed answers. Ask questions about anything that still puzzles or intrigues you.

Do you need to go over key terms and ideas from any one of the previous activities before moving on to the next part of the challenge?

 E *Sonnet recital* **1–2 hours**

application

1

Now you have an opportunity to show your knowledge and appreciation of sonnets. Choose one of the two tasks below.

★ Study and recite a sonnet by a famous poet.

★ Write and recite a sonnet of your own.

Be prepared to explain either your choice of poem or the choices that you made in writing your sonnet.

Help

Whichever task you choose you should aim to learn your poem and perform it from memory. See Resources box 3 for sites that will tell you about techniques for memorising. You could also perform your sonnet as a piece of drama or support your performance with a PowerPoint demonstration. You could even sing it; after all, sonnets were known as 'little songs'! If necessary, get some classmates to aid your performance by taking roles or by helping with equipment. They could also proof-read your poem for you.

Try to help your audience grasp as much meaning from your sonnets as possible. Vary your tone of voice and use gestures to emphasise images and ideas. Do the same when you explain your poems afterwards.

If you want to find a sonnet to recite

Search your school or classroom libraries for poetry anthologies. Ask your teacher if you can look in the cupboards in the English department. You could also visit the sites listed in Resources box 3. If you are not choosing a sonnet by Shakespeare or one of the ones from the websites, do check your choice with your teacher to make sure that you are studying a worthwhile poem.

If you want to write your own sonnet

If you want ideas for what to write about, look at the notes that you made in Activity A. You could also visit the websites in the Resources box and look again at what subjects famous poets chose.

Alternatively, you could photocopy and cut up several sonnets by Shakespeare, identify good rhyming words and rearrange them to form your own pastiche (imitation) of a Shakespearean sonnet!

Whatever you do, remember to observe the rules of the sonnet form. If you decide to break any rules, you should do so consciously.

Resources 3

Sonnet sites

Here are a number of sites that will provide you with sonnets that are easy to search for and print. Milton and Meredith are included because they had sonnet forms named after them. Other poets have been chosen for the quality of their sonnets and their potential for dramatic performance.

John Keats (1795–1821)
http://www.sonnets.org/keats.htm#010

John Clare (1793–1864)
http://www.sonnets.org/clare.htm

Leigh Hunt (1784–1859)
http://www.sonnets.org/hunt.htm#100

John Milton (1608–74)
http://www.sonnets.org/milton.htm

Christina Rossetti (1830–94)
http://www.sonnets.org/rossettc.htm

George Meredith (1828–1909)
http://www.sonnets.org/meredith.htm

Robert Burns (1759–96)
http://www.sonnets.org/burns.htm

William Wordsworth (1770–1850)
http://www.sonnets.org/wordsworth.htm

Sonnets of the First World War (1914–18)
http://www.sonnets.org/wwi.htm

Algernon Charles Swinburn (1837–1909)
http://www.sonnets.org/swinburn.htm

Memory sites

To help you prepare for your recital of a poem, it may help to learn a few memory techniques. Remember to choose a technique that will suit your learning style. Impress your friends with magical feats of memory by visiting:

Mnemonic Techniques and Specific Memory Tricks
http://brain.web-us.com/memory/mnemonic_techniques.htm

Memory Improvement.co.uk
http://www.memoryweb.freeuk.com/?hop=ashbury.forgepress

Information

Here is some excellent advice on how to memorise poetry by one of Britain's foremost poets, the late Ted Hughes.

Ted Hughes wrote a fascinating afterword on 'Memorising Poems' in an anthology that he jointly edited with Seamus Heaney in 1997, called *The Rattle Bag*. Hughes' advice is to use chains of images to remember lines and he gives an extended example of how to do this.

There are many reasons for learning poems. But memorising them should be like a game. It should be a pleasure […]

One of the brain's spontaneous techniques for fixing anything in the conscious memory, in other words for making it easy to recall, is to connect it with a vivid visual image. And the more absurd, exaggerated, grotesque that image is, the more unforgettable is the thing to which we connect it. One easy technique for memorising poems uses visualised images in this way.

Basically, this particular technique is good for memorising lists. For example:

A peaty burn (stream)
A brown horse
An avalanche
A roaring lion
A hen-coop
A comb
A fleece
Foam
A flute
A lake
Home

might be dealt with as follows:

For 'peaty burn' it might be enough simply to imagine, like a frame in a colour film, a dark torrential mountain stream coming down among boulders. But to make sure it is 'burn' and not 'stream' that you remember, it might be better to remember the stream actually burning, sending up flames and smoke: a cascade of dark fire, scorching the banks.

The next item, 'brown horse', now has to be connected to the burning stream. The most obvious shortcut is to put the horse in the torrent of fire, trying to scramble out – possibly with its mane in flames.

The next item, 'avalanche', now has to be connected to the brown horse. One easy solution would be to imagine the stream as an avalanche, with the horse galloping among the big rolling rocks, its mane smoking.

The next item, 'a roaring lion', has to be connected to the avalanche. The torrent of boulders could be imagined pouring down onto the head of a huge sleepy lion, who wakes up shaking them from his mane, and roaring.

The next item, 'a hen-coop', has to be connected to that lion. Again the short cut is to jam the lion inside the hen-coop – perhaps chewing the hen.

The next item, 'a comb', has to be connected to the coop. The lion has burst from the coop and gone. So now you construct a rickety, awkward, great comb out of the splintered slats of the hen-coop – try combing your own hair with it.

And so on. If each image is 'photographed' mentally, as on a screen, it will not be forgotten easily. And each image will bring on the next, which has been connected to it. Even when you are remembering a very long list, the procedure is quite small-scale and automatic, because you are never remembering more than one connection at a time, and each connection provides you with the next. The rolling rocks produce – surprise – the lion. The lion produces – out of nowhere, and against all expectations – the hen coop. The hen produces – can it be right? – the ridiculous wooden comb.

Theoretically, if each connecting image is visualised successfully, the list can be endless, because each step will always produce the next.

The same technique is used by professional memorisers for memorising poems. Some readers might have recognised the list above. The first two lines of Hopkins' poem 'Inversnaid' go:

> This darksome burn, horseback brown,
> His rollrock highroad roaring down'

[…] Some may meet a difficulty in releasing the imagination enough to produce the visual images for the cartoon. But practice helps. The release of playful imagination also releases energy, and the brain soon becomes skilful at what it enjoys […]

Memory techniques of the kind I have described, using strongly visualised imagery, were invented in the ancient world and became the basis of learning in the Christian Middle Ages, when books were scarce […]

In England in the seventeenth century, the Puritan/Protestant ascendancy of the Civil War made a serious bid to eradicate imagery from all aspects of life – methodically destroying the religious imagery of churches and forbidding the imaginative play of drama. The same spirit also banished from the schools the old-established memory techniques that used 'imagery' and officially replaced them with 'learning by rote'. The discarded methods, dimly associated with paganism and Catholicism, were soon forgotten. […] 'Learning by rote' became the norm.

From *The Rattle Bag*, edited by Seamus Heaney and Ted Hughes

If you would like to know more, find and read the whole of Ted Hughes' 'Afterword'.

evaluation

1 Here is a fun way to evaluate the performance of classmates and still reinforce some of the key targets in this challenge. However your own individual review at the end of this challenge will count for far more.

Score out of five and add the total for a score.

Award points from 1–5	OK 1	Good 2	Very good 3	Excellent 4	On another planet 5	Score
The format of the sonnet.	It has 14 lines.	It has the correct rhyme schemes and syllable length.	It has an appropriate format and structure.	It also uses impressive imagery and a well-known theme.	It also has striking use of form, skilful diction and imagery.	
The student's performance: did their recital help the audience's understanding of the poem?	Sound but not inspiring; not enough variation of pitch or tone.	Quite expressive: captured the audience's interest with body language.	Expressive and used rhythm and gestures to reveal form.	Very expressive: used rhythm, gestures or drama to express form.	Highly expressive: used rhythm, gestures or drama to convey form.	
Reasons given for either writing or selecting the sonnet; explanation of the poem.	Simple reasons for choices made. A basic explanation.	Reasonably good reasons for choices made. Explained the poem reasonably well.	Very thoughtful reasons for choices made. Well explained.	Excellent reasons for choices made. Very well explained.	Outstanding reasons for choices made. Brilliantly explained.	

evaluation

2 Consider the views of your audience who commented on the quality of your sonnet and your performance in reciting it. Do you think that their comments were valid? How much of this challenge have you been able to accomplish?

You may, as a class, wish to spend some time comparing your work by displaying it and discussing how things went.

Fill in the assessment grid as part of your evidence for your portfolio.

How confident are you that you achieved the aims of this challenge?

Aim achieved	Not very confident	Reasonably confident	Confident	Very confident
I can identify every type of sonnet.				
I can explain how they are constructed.				
I understand how sonnets developed over time.				
I was able to analyse or compose a sonnet and recite it.				

If you ticked any of the boxes in the first column of the grid, go back over the relevant sections of this assignment. Clarify your ideas and think through what you know about sonnets so you can improve your overall understanding of them.

Next steps

Are there any sonnets or poets that touched upon issues that you would like to explore further?

The form lends itself to chains of poems. One poet, for instance, has written a sonnet for each month of the year. Could you write a chain of sonnets on a connected theme or idea?

Look at other forms of poetry, for example ballads or elegies. What are the main features of these types of poetry? How are they constructed? What patterns of language do they have? How have poets used or adapted their forms over time?

Integrity and corruption in A Man For All Seasons

Target

This challenge will enable you to:

★ gain an understanding of Sir Thomas More's life and times (early 1500s)

★ appreciate how Robert Bolt uses this historical setting to reflect events in his own time (1960s)

★ appreciate More's role as a teacher in the play

★ understand More's sense of selfhood and his refusal to change

★ understand how the 'Common Man' represents the compromises that most people have to make in their lives

★ appreciate how personal ambition for power and position can easily lead to compromise and corruption.

About this assignment

This assignment links to other subjects in the curriculum. Your work may incorporate:

★ art   ★ drama
★ history   ★ ICT
★ music   ★ RE

Learning styles

For each activity, consider how you might work in the learning style that suits you best:

★ auditory   ★ kinaesthetic   ★ visual   ★ any combination of these.

A   *The background to the play*   **1–2 hours**

knowledge

1   Choose *one* of the following activities. Whichever you do, write up your research in the form of linear notes, a spidergram or a poster.

<u>Either</u> find out about the play's historical context

Find out about the historical setting of *A Man For All Seasons*. What important ideas, issues and events were taking place in England during the 1520s–30s?

Find and listen to some of the music of the period. What does it sound like and what effect do you think it had on audiences at the time? What were the lyrics of songs generally about?

<u>Or</u> find out about important historical events from the playwright's time

Robert Bolt wrote *A Man For All Seasons* in the 1960s. What big ideas, issues and events concerned people in Britain and around the world at that time? Can any links be made with the period in which the play is set? Why do you think Robert Bolt wrote this particular play at that time?

Resources 1

Your school library may have some helpful modern history books, collections of magazines, encyclopaedias and reference books to aid your research.

Here are some websites to help with your search for information on the historical background to the play.

History and the 1500s

Bamber Gascoigne's *History World* is an excellent website for historical research. It is worth trying the site's search engine and then taking the *England History Tour*. Click through the historical events to Henry VIII and Sir Thomas More. Do not forget to press all the brown link buttons to get further information when you take a tour.
www.historyworld.net/

Tudor England 1485–1603
www.englishhistory.net/tudor.html

Britannia History
The best *A Man For All Seasons* study site
http://home.pacific.net.au/~greg.hub/seasons.html

History and the 1960s

Modern History (click on the 1960s)
www.information-entertainment.com/History/

Google Web Directory: Twentieth Century
http://directory.google.com/Top/Society/History/By_Time_Period/Twentieth_Century/

2 Each pair presents the main findings from their research in a whole-class discussion.

Spend about 20 minutes discussing your findings as a class. Listen carefully to presentations about the activity that you did not do and make a note of the most important facts and ideas. Make a note of any new information that you think will be useful for achieving the main aims of this challenge.

B   *Read* A Man for All Seasons

90 minutes

1 Read the following extract from *A Man For All Seasons*. (Underline any words that you do not know and look them up in a good dictionary.)

Sir Thomas More (Paul Scofield) talking to Richard Rich (John Hurt) in a scene from the 1966 film version of *A Man For All Seasons* directed by Fred Zinnemann.

When the curtain rises, the set is in darkness but for a single spot which descends vertically upon the COMMON MAN, who stands in front of a big property basket.

COMMON MAN: It is perverse! To start a play made up of Kings and Cardinals in speaking costumes and intellectuals with embroidered mouths, with me.

If a King, or a Cardinal had done the prologue he'd have had the right materials. And an intellectual would have shown enough majestic meanings, coloured propositions, and closely woven liturgical stuff to dress the House of Lords! But this!

Is this a costume? Does this say anything? It barely covers one man's nakedness! A bit of black material to reduce Old Adam to the Common Man.

Oh, if they'd let me come on naked, I could have shown you something of my own. Which would have told you without words—! . . . Something I've forgotten . . . Old Adam's muffled up.

(Backing towards basket.) Well, for a proposition of my own, I need a costume. *(Takes out and puts on the coat and hat of STEWARD.)*

Matthew! The Household Steward of Sir Thomas More!

(Lights come up swiftly on set. He takes from the basket five silver goblets, one larger than the others, and a jug with a lid with which he furnishes the table. A burst of conversational merriment off; he pauses and indicates head of stairs.) There's company to dinner. *(Finishes business at table.)*

All Right! A Common Man! A Sixteenth-Century Butler! *(He drinks from the jug.)* All right – the Six—*(Breaks off, agreeably surprised by the quality of the liquor, regards the jug respectfully and drinks again.)* The Sixteenth Century is the Century of the Common Man. *(Puts down the jug.)* Like all the other centuries. *(Crossing right.)* And that's my proposition.

During the last part of the speech, voices off. Now, enter, at head of stairs, SIR THOMAS MORE.

STEWARD:	That's Sir Thomas More.
MORE:	The wine please, Matthew?
STEWARD:	It's there, Sir Thomas.

MORE (*looking into the jug*): Is it good?

STEWARD: Bless you, sir! I don't know.

MORE (*mildly*): Bless you too, Matthew.

Enter RICH *at head of stairs.*

RICH (*enthusiastically pursuing an argument*):
But every man has his price!

STEWARD (*contemptuous*): Master Richard Rich.

RICH: But yes! In money too.

MORE (*gentle impatience*): No no no.

RICH: Or pleasure. Titles, women, bricks-and-mortar, there's always something.

MORE: Childish.

RICH: Well, in suffering, certainly.

MORE (*interested*): Buy a man with suffering?

RICH: Impose suffering, and offer him – escape.

MORE: Oh. For a moment I thought you were being profound. (*Gives cup to RICH.*)

RICH (*to STEWARD*): Good evening, Matthew.

STEWARD (*snubbing*): 'Evening, sir.

RICH: No, not a bit profound; it then becomes a purely practical question of how to make him suffer sufficiently.

MORE: Mm. . . .(*Takes him by the arm and walks with him.*) And . . . who recommended you to read Signor Machiavelli?

(*RICH breaks away laughing; a fraction too long. MORE smiles.*) No, who? (*More laughter.*) . . .Mm?

RICH: Master Cromwell.

MORE: Oh . . . (*Back to the wine jug and cups.*) He's a very able man.

RICH:	And so he is!
MORE:	Yes, I say he is. He's very able.
RICH:	And he will do something for me, he says.
MORE:	I didn't know you knew him.
RICH:	Pardon me, Sir Thomas, but how much do you know about me?
MORE:	Whatever you've let me know.
RICH:	I've let you know everything!
MORE:	Richard, you should go back to Cambridge; you're deteriorating.
RICH:	Well, I'm not used! . . . D'you know how much I have to show for seven months' work—
MORE:	Work?
RICH:	– Work! Waiting's work when you wait as I wait, hard! . . . For seven months, that's two hundred days, I have to show: the acquaintance of the Cardinal's outer doorman, the indifference of the Cardinal's inner doorman, and the Cardinal's chamberlain's hand in my chest! . . . Oh – also one half of a Good Morning delivered at fifty paces by the Duke of Norfolk. Doubtless he mistook me for someone.
MORE:	He was very affable at dinner.
RICH:	Oh. Everyone's affable *here*. . . . *(MORE is pleased.)* Also, of course, the friendship of Sir Thomas More. Or should I say acquaintance?
MORE:	Say friendship.
RICH:	Well there! 'A friend of Sir Thomas and still no office? There must be something wrong with him.'
MORE:	I thought we said friendship. . . . *(Considers; then)* The Dean of St Paul's offers you a post; with a house, a servant and fifty pounds a year.
RICH:	What? What post?

MORE:	At the new school.
RICH (*bitterly disappointed*):	A teacher!
MORE:	A man should go where he won't be tempted. Look, Richard, see this. (*Hands a silver cup.*) Look. . . . Look. . . .
RICH:	Beautiful.
MORE:	Italian. . . . Do you want it?
RICH:	Why—?
MORE:	No joke; keep it; sell it.
RICH:	Well I— Thank you of course—Thank you! Thank you! But—?
MORE:	You'll sell it, won't you?
RICH:	Yes, I think so. Yes, I will.
MORE:	And buy, what?
RICH (*sudden ferocity*):	Some decent clothes!
MORE (*with sympathy*):	Ah.
RICH:	I want a gown like yours.
MORE:	You'll get several gowns for that I should think. It was sent to me a little while ago by some woman. Now she's put a lawsuit into the Court of Requests. It's a bribe, Richard.
RICH:	Oh . . . (*Chagrined.*) So you give it away of course.
MORE:	Yes!
RICH:	To me?
MORE:	We'll, I'm not going to keep it, and you need it. Of course – if you feel it's contaminated . . .
RICH:	No no. I'll risk it. (*Both smile.*)
MORE:	But Richard, in office they offer you all sorts of things. I was once offered a whole village, with a mill, and a manor house, and heaven knows what else – a coat of arms I shouldn't be surprised. Why not be a teacher?

	You'd be a fine teacher. Perhaps, a great one.
RICH:	And if I was who would know it?
MORE:	You, your pupils, your friends, God. Not a bad public, that. . . . Oh, and a *quiet* life.
RICH *(laughing)*:	You say that!
MORE:	Richard, I was commanded into office; it was inflicted on me. . . . *(RICH regards him.)* Can't you believe that?
RICH:	It's hard.
MORE *(grimly)*:	Be a teacher.

Extract from *A Man For All Seasons*, Act 1

analysis

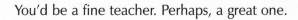

2 Read the text once more then use it to help you with the following questions. You do not have to answer every question, but make sure that your research includes some work at each level. As you work, note down any other points you would like to make or questions you would like to ask about this extract.

Text level

★ Sum up in one or two paragraphs what happens in this extract.

★ What role or roles do you think the Common Man plays?

★ Why does Sir Thomas More want Master Rich to 'be a teacher'?

★ In what ways could More himself be seen as a teacher in relation to Master Rich?

★ From this extract, what do you think is the main moral or lesson of the play?

★ How do you think that each of the three characters who appear in this scene will change or develop through the play?

★ Robert Bolt says in his preface that More had an 'adamantine sense of his own self'. Given your knowledge of the extract, and perhaps the play, what do you think Bolt means by this?

Sentence level

✦ In this extract, each character puts forward several propositions or arguments. Explain, as fully as you can, what the characters are saying in each of the following speeches.

a) THE COMMON MAN: All Right! A Common Man! A Sixteenth-Century Butler! *(He drinks from the jug.)* All right – the Six—*(Breaks off, agreeably surprised by the quality of the liquor, regards the jug respectfully and drinks again.)* The Sixteenth Century is the Century of the Common Man. *(Puts down the jug.)* Like all the other centuries. *(Crossing right.)* And that's my proposition.

b) RICH *(enthusiastically pursuing an argument)*: But every man has his price!

c) MORE: A man should go where he won't be tempted. Look, Richard, see this. *(Hands a silver cup.)* Look . . . Look . . .

✦ Robert Bolt may have drawn the play's title from Desiderius Erasmus' description of More as 'a man for all hours' from Erasmus' work *In Praise of Folly*, which was inspired by his friendship with More and written in 1509. Erasmus admired More for his strong sense of self and his unchanging outlook on life. Why do you think that Bolt called his play, *A Man For All Seasons*?

✦ From the context of the conversation between Sir Thomas More and Master Rich, what is explicitly stated and what is inferred about Master Cromwell?

✦ What is More trying to teach Rich by offering him the silver cup?

✦ What does Master Rich want above all else?

✦ How does Bolt create a realistic conversation in the extract between More and Rich? (Think about the way each character's speech is represented.)

✦ What is your opinion of the advice More gives Rich about being 'a teacher'?

Word level

✦ Select some words and phrases from the stage directions for each of three characters in this extract. Explain how these words or phrases would help an audience understand the nature, motives or inner life of each character.

✦ Choose one word or phrase from the extract that best sums up each character and give a reason for each of your choices.

synthesis

3

Spend several minutes checking through your answers with a partner. You may need to check some of the answers against the extract to sort out your ideas and deepen your understanding. Clarify your answers and ideas as far as possible before you engage in a whole-class discussion.

evaluation

4

The whole-class discussion is another opportunity to extend your notes and clarify your ideas. Remember that you can ask questions too!

Make a note of any fresh points or ideas that you may need to follow up with further research before going on to the next task. For more active research you should frame these points and ideas as questions.

 C *Read the play*   **2–3 hours**

comprehension

  1

As a class, agree a method for reading the play. There are a number of suggestions for different ways of doing this on Worksheet 15.

As you read the play, pause where necessary to think about the themes listed below and answer some of the questions. Your notes can take the form of spidergrams or linear notes with headings and bullet points if you prefer.

More's role as a teacher in the play

★ What does More teach other characters and why does he teach them? Look at his conversations with:

a) William Roper (on the law near the end of Act 1)

b) the Duke of Norfolk (on their friendship in Act 2)

c) his daughter, Margaret (on oaths and the state in Act 2 when she visits More, jailed in The Tower of London).

More's sense of selfhood and his refusal to change

★ What are the principles that More sticks to and why does he do so?

★ Near the end of Act 1, during his conversation with William Roper on the laws of England, Thomas More uses an extended seafaring metaphor of ships, water and anchors. Reread the passage and explain what More means by his imagery.

The role of the Common Man

★ Who does the Common Man represent?

★ Give a few examples of how the Common Man makes the compromises that most of us make in our daily lives to get by.

★ In what ways can you identify with him? (Remember that there are also at least two female characters that play the same kind of role: A Woman from Act 2 and, perhaps to a lesser degree, More's wife, Alice.)

The idea that 'every man has his price'

★ Several characters are corrupted by power and position in this play. Identify at least two of them and give detailed explanations for your choice.

Resources 2

The website below provides excellent support for this assignment and may help you to clarify your ideas, confirm answers or simply find out more about the text. The website is extensive so be prepared for a long visit!

The best *A Man For All Seasons* study site
http://home.pacific.net.au/~greg.hub/seasons.html

Break off from your reading at regular intervals to write your notes and to discuss your understanding of conversations, events and themes in the play. As this is your first reading you will need to do this every six pages or so. (But use your common sense and do not break in the middle of an important conversation between characters.) You can, if necessary, always reread parts of the play to find the information that you need for your notes.

From time to time your teacher will hold whole-class discussions on the play. Set out your notes as prompts beforehand so you can play a full part in these discussions.

 D *From stage to screen* 3–4 hours

comprehension

 1

In 1966 Fred Zinnemann produced and directed a highly acclaimed film version of *A Man For All Seasons*, scripted by Robert Bolt. There was also a made-for-TV film version in 1988, directed by and starring Charlton Heston.

If possible, watch the Zinnemann film version. Compare the screen adaptation with Bolt's original play and think about how the medium of film led Bolt to make some changes in the play. Use the following questions as starting points.

★ Dramatically, what is lost or gained by changing the order of some events in Act 1?

★ Are there parts of the play where the medium of film allows an audience to see what cannot be represented on stage? Give some examples.

★ Why do you think that in the film version Bolt alters the role of Common Man and leaves out certain characters such as Chapuys?

★ Compare the two endings that Bolt wrote for his stage play with the ending of the film version. Which ending do you think is the most effective? Give reasons for your answer.

2 Once you have read the entire play, discuss as a class these main themes:

★ More's sense of selfhood and his refusal to change

★ Thomas's role as a teacher

★ the Common Man and who and what he represents

★ personal ambition and power and how some characters are corrupted by them.

Discuss also any other issues, points and ideas that came up as you read the play.

Help

Different interpretations of the same text

Make a note of any unusual interpretations of the text and its themes and ideas presented by other pupils. Interpretations of literature can vary and this is one of the reasons why the subject is so interesting. Different people may latch on to and explore different aspects of characterisation in a text and you may find that people in your class come up with different answers to the same questions! Just remember that whatever point someone makes, they need to back it with evidence (brief quotations and so forth). If there is textual evidence that supports the point, then they have a case. Of course, you do not have to agree with anyone else's interpretation or answer if you prefer your own. But try to weigh different arguments fairly and be prepared to give way if someone else has a better case than you.

Add to the notes that you have already made on each topic. Carry out further research to clarify your ideas if you need to.

Now try a creative exercise that draws on your knowledge of the play. You could choose a task that suits your intelligence or learning style; alternatively you could pick one that will help you improve a weaker intelligence. Your finished product should be presented to a real audience such as your classmates or year group.

Auditory tasks

Most of these activities will need some planning and writing up first! Try a mind map or bubble diagram to set out your ideas.

★ Hot seating. Find out all you can about one of the main characters in the play. Look at their motivation, what other characters think of them, what they say or do and how they change during the play. To present, allow the class to quiz you in role for about 10 minutes.

★ Alter ego (paired activity). Choose a monologue or dialogue from the play and explore the 'real person' behind the lines. Decide what the character might be thinking as well as the subtext or implications of what they actually say. To present, one student takes the role and speaks the dialogue, pausing at the end of each line or sentence. The other person stands behind the 'actor' as the 'alter ego' and says what the character is really thinking. Each character will need two students to carry out this activity.

★ Choose a character and consider what thoughts they might have at the end of the play and what they might feel about the decisions they made at various points in the action. Present your work as a short monologue, with the character reminiscing about events.

★ Write an extra scene in which characters discuss More's strong sense of selfhood and his inability to change his mind on the key issue of Henry VIII's new marriage.

★ Pair up with another student and write a dialogue in which two of the play's characters meet five days, five weeks or five years after the action. Their discussion centres on their decisions, motives and actions.

Visual-linguistic tasks

★ Write a solicitor's brief for a lawyer defending More in the court case. You could refer to More's use of 'silence' and his strong sense of conscience and selfhood.

- Write More's final letter to his family or to a friend the night before his execution, justifying the decisions that he made.

- Write a monologue with More talking to the audience about his conscience and the reasons why he could not change his mind over the marriage.

Resources 3

For information about More's trial and legal briefs in general.

Duhaime.Org: The Trial of Sir Thomas More, 1535
http://www.duhaime.org/uk-more.htm

Brief Reporter
http://www.briefreporter.com/

Visual-spatial tasks

- Design a set for an important scene in the play. Show where characters would stand as they deliver particular speeches. Include props that could symbolise the play's themes, ideas and characterisation.

- Write and design a programme for the play. Include the cover, background information, casting and scenes. Try to include some of the themes referred to in this challenge. If you can, look at a theatre programme first for further ideas.

- Draw or paint a scene or an event from the play. Try to find ways of representing some of the play's main themes in your picture, as well as any other themes and ideas that you noticed in your reading of the play.

Kinaesthetic tasks

- Adapt and play the opening scene with updated characters and settings. For example, the new setting could be a merchant bank or a firm of lawyers and King Henry could be the company's managing director. Try to emphasise Bolt's themes of integrity, ambition and corruption in your new version. (You will need to work with like-minded students to perform this activity.)

- Improvise a scene or a conversation that takes place outside the action of the play, perhaps one referred to by other characters. For example, you could create a scene with a different conversation between More and Common Man in another of his guises.

- Create one or more freeze frames for a significant part of the play. Capture your freeze frames on camera and then present the images to an audience, explaining the significance of each one.

evaluation

  2

Reflect as a class on your achievements and what you learned from the various presentations. Help others by giving feedback; point out what you think they did well and give suggestions for what could have been improved.

Update your notes where necessary for a fuller understanding of the main aims of this challenge. Make a note of any points or issues arising out of other students' work that you would like to clarify or research further.

F *Evaluation* | 20 minutes

evaluation

  1

Fill in the assessment grid and add it to the notes and work from this assignment that you already have in your portfolio.

Aim achieved	Not very confident	Reasonably confident	Confident	Very confident
I understand the historical background of the play.				
I can appreciate More's role as a teacher in the play.				
I understand More's sense of selfhood and his refusal to change.				
I could appreciate the daily compromises of Common Man.				
I can see how personal ambition for power and position can easily lead to compromise and corruption.				

Next steps

Find out about a modern example of a man or woman with a strong conscience or sense of self. Choose someone who has suffered injustice or great hardship because they refused to compromise their values and beliefs. It could be:

* Nelson Mandela

* Martin Luther King

* Aung San Suu Kyi

* Mahatma Gandhi

* Mother Teresa

* someone else chosen by you.

Explain the contribution that this person has made to their own society and how they are perceived by the world. You could go on to explain how your choice of person is different from Bolt's Common Man.

Explore rites and rituals in three modern poems

Target

This challenge will enable you to:

★ develop your skills of poetry appreciation

★ examine how poets from different cultures approach similar themes

★ make a detailed comparison of how two modern poems treat the same theme

★ produce a creative or analytical piece of work on rites and rituals.

About this assignment

This assignment links to other subjects in the curriculum. Your work may incorporate:

★ art   ★ drama
★ ICT   ★ music
★ RE

Learning styles

For each activity, consider how you might work in the learning style that suits you best:

★ auditory   ★ kinaesthetic   ★ visual   ★ any combination of these.

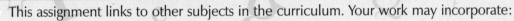

 A   *Explore rites and rituals across different cultures*

10 minutes

knowledge

1   Read the following information on rites and rituals very carefully.

! Information

A definition of rites and rituals

A *rite* is a solemn religious or social observance.

A *ritual* is a set of prescribed actions that usually takes place in a particular order to perform a rite. Rituals usually involve a number of symbols that represent ideas. They have a social purpose within a specific culture.

Various kinds of rites and rituals

The most common rites and rituals practised by most cultures are connected with:

* initiation or rites of passage: these mark new stages in life or admittance to groups within society. They may involve a mock death and rebirth to enact the change as, for example, in baptism.

* instruction: to gain new spiritual knowledge or experience

* sacrifice: in many cultures this means purging oneself of some unwanted habit or trait in the expectation of becoming a better person. This might be done, for example, through fasting, as in Lent and Ramadan.

* devotion: prayers and religious observances

* seasonal celebration: the observance and participation in special days and festivals to celebrate the changing seasons

* consecration: blessing things or setting them apart as special. It could involve books, houses, people and objects.

* anathemas and banishment: the cleansing of something or someone from evil spirits, as for example, in exorcism

* other special occasions: this includes commemorations, weddings, birthdays, family occasions, sporting or other events, for example the opening ceremony at the Olympic Games.

In each category you would find many examples of rites and rituals from a wide variety of different cultures. Some, such as the Olympic Games ceremony, are large public occasions; others, such as birthdays and weddings, are personal or family events.

knowledge

 2 List ten rites that are practised in your culture. Briefly describe the purpose of, and rituals used for, each rite.

synthesis

 3 Discuss your lists in small groups, adding notes if you need to include more detail. Make a note of any rites that you found interesting or had not heard of before. You may wish to investigate them further.

4

Explore this topic further in a whole-class discussion. Note that the number and variety of rites and rituals may vary depending on the range of cultures that are represented within your class.

B *Investigate two rites and rituals*   **1 hour**

knowledge

 1

Research two different rites or rituals practised in a different culture to your own. Write some brief notes on them and find some pictures or symbols that you can use as props to support your feedback in a whole-class discussion. Your notes could be in either linear or in spidergram form.

Resources 1

As well as visiting your school or local library, you could talk to family or friends who are from, or have experience of, a different culture.

Here are a few websites that may also help with your research.

MJOE: coming of age in other cultures
http://www.mjoe.org/cultures/index.php

Trance and Shamanism: healing rituals among traditional cultures
http://www.purabudaya.com/News/imaginaire/trance.htm

World Death Rituals
http://death.monstrous.com/death_rituals_across_cultures_.htm

Religious Rituals
http://www.wrkfl.com/id45.htm

evaluation

 2

Discuss your research as a class. Write notes on any interesting or unusual contributions from other pupils. Ask questions on aspects of rites and rituals that you would like to know more about.

knowledge

1 Read the poem 'Sacrifice' several times.

Sacrifice

As he moves the knife across the neck of the goat
I can feel its point on my throat;
And as the blood geysers from the jugular,
A hot and sticky sweat breaks out on my body.

We are laying the foundations of a friend's house.
After a brief prayer that all who dwell here
May be blessed, we stand in a tight circle
Around the animal to be sacrificed; it has
A civilized and patient look. The glare of the sun,
The heat, and the smell of blood make me dizzy.

The knife is with my friend; it is a necessary
Part of the ritual that it is his hand only
Which should draw the blood. How keenly it cuts!
The movement is a little unsteady, perhaps,
But forgive him, this is his first butchering.
Four calloused hands imprison my jerking legs.

The children are fascinated by the tableau,
And watch in satisfaction the blood flow
Into the hastily dug hole. Two spadefuls of dirt
Will cover me up for ever. A white-bearded man
Chants something holy, and feebly thrusts the pick
Into the virgin ground; the cameras click.

We are not laying the foundations of a house,
But another Dachau.

Taufiq Rafat

analysis

2 With a partner work through the text, sentence and word-level questions. You do not have to answer every question, but make sure that you include some work at each level.

Text level

★ What kind of rite is taking place in this poem?

★ Where would you place the cultural context of the poem?

★ How and why does the narrator change in this poem?

★ Identify the form of the poem and explain why you think it is appropriate.

★ Give your views on the poem.

Sentence level

★ What kind of narrator speaks this text? Why is this kind of narrator particularly effective?

★ Select the lines or images that had most impact for you and give reasons for your choices.

★ How does the poet's use of caesuras (breaks or pauses, which are made here by punctuation) add expressive meaning to the poem?

★ An envoi (from the French for 'message') is the last part of a poem that gives the poet's summary or conclusion. What is implied in the envoi of this poem?

★ What would you say is the poem's tone?

Word level

★ Make a list of words that refer to rites and rituals. How do they help set the poem's mood or tone?

★ Identify some of the alliteration or onomatopoeia used in the poem and say why you think they were used.

★ What is implied by the goat's 'civilized and patient look'?

★ Which words seem to reveal the narrator's disapproval of this rite? Give reasons for your choices.

★ Make notes on any points or ideas in the poem that interested you or you would like to know more about.

evaluation

3 After checking your answers with your partner, discuss your answers as a class. Make notes on points that clarify any questions you were unsure about. Reread the text again if you to need to revise your ideas. Your work on this poem will help you with the next task in this assignment.

Revise your knowledge of poetic technique

Use Worksheet 17 to revise a number of common poetic terms before working on the main task in this section. Scan each poem very carefully and see how the poets add meaning through their use of poetic technique.

1 You are going to compare two poems from different cultures. First, form a small group and read the following poems several times, making notes as you go or using a pencil to annotate the poems for meaning as you read them. You can, if you wish, include 'Sacrifice' as one of the poems for your study. .

'Night of the Scorpion'

I remember the night my mother
was stung by a scorpion. Ten hours
of steady rain had driven him
to crawl beneath a sack of rice.
Parting with his poison – flash
of diabolic tail in the dark room –
he risked the rain again.
The peasants came like swarms of flies
and buzzed the name of God a hundred times
to paralyse the Evil One.

With candles and with lanterns
throwing giant scorpion shadows
on the mud-baked walls
they searched for him: he was not found.
They clicked their tongues.
With every movement that the scorpion made
his poison moved in Mother's blood, they said.
May he sit still, they said.
May the sins of your previous birth
be burned away tonight, they said.
May your suffering decrease
the misfortunes of your next birth, they said.
May the sum of evil
balanced in this unreal world
against the sum of good
become diminished by your pain.
May the poison purify your flesh
of desire, and your spirit of ambition,
they said, and they sat around
on the floor with my mother in the centre,
the peace of understanding on each face.
More candles, more lanterns, more neighbours,
more insects, and the endless rain.
My mother twisted through and through,
groaning on a mat.
My father, sceptic, rationalist,
trying every curse and blessing,
powder, mixture, herb and hybrid.
He even poured a little paraffin
upon the bitten toe and put a match to it.
I watched the flame feeding on my mother.
I watched the holy man perform his rites
to tame the poison with an incantation.
After twenty hours
it lost its sting.

My mother only said
Thank God the scorpion picked on me
and spared my children.

Nissim Ezekiel from *Latter Day Psalms*

Explore rites and rituals in three modern poems

'Mid-Term Break'

I sat all morning in the college sick bay
Counting bells knelling classes to a close.
At two o'clock our neighbours drove me home.

In the porch I met my father crying–
He had always taken funerals in his stride–
And Big Jim Evans saying it was a hard blow.

The baby cooed and laughed and rocked the pram
When I came in, and I was embarrassed
By old men standing up to shake my hand

And tell me they were "sorry for my trouble",
Whispers informed strangers I was the eldest,
Away at school, as my mother held my hand

In hers and coughed out angry tearless sighs.
At ten o'clock the ambulance arrived
With the corpse, stanched and bandaged by the nurses.

Next morning I went up into the room. Snowdrops
And candles soothed the bedside; I saw him
For the first time in six weeks. Paler now,

Wearing a poppy bruise on his left temple,
He lay in the four foot box as in his cot.
No gaudy scars, the bumper knocked him clear.

A four foot box, a foot for every year.

From Death of A Naturalist – New Selected Poems, by Seamus Heaney

analysis

 2 Use your notes to help you begin comparing the two poems. Use the following
questions to help you.

	Poem 1	Poem 2
Briefly explain what each poem is about.		
How does the first-person narrator see other people in the poem?		

	Poem 1	Poem 2
What rites and rituals does the poem describe?		
What do they reveal about the culture?		
Identify some of the poetic techniques that the poet uses and explain how they add meaning to the poem.		
What is each poem's form and how does it complement the poem's subject matter?		
Identify words and phrases that reveal each poem's mood and tone.		
What are your views on each poem?		

Information

Form in poetry

Remember that poets use form to add to the meaning or mood of a poem.

For instance:

★ Ezekiel uses repetition to give a sense of the ritualistic chants of the peasants.

★ Heaney likes to use run-on lines and stanzas to 'enact' people's actions. For example, 'my mother held my hand / In hers', where the space between the lines helps to emphasise the rhythmic action of holding hands. This is also a symbolic image of grief before the non-family mourners at Heaney's dead brother's wake.

The form in Heaney's poem, unrhymed tercets, is rare in English poetry. The form normally lends itself to humorous, fast paced poems. Heaney only allows one line to run freely – and that describes the baby's innocence. Instead of the usual and more harmonious eight stanzas, Heaney uses seven. Why do you think he does this?

3 Discuss and agree your points and ideas within your group. Appoint a spokesperson for your group and offer your ideas in the whole-class discussion.

Write notes on any points and ideas that you find interesting or that your group had not thought of. Much poetry is open to a wide range of interpretation. Did everyone agree on these poems or were there differences in interpretation? Not everyone thinks alike! Reread the texts if you need to clarify or change your points and answers.

E *Present your interpretation*

 1–2 hours

 1 Choose one of the following tasks and then explain or present your work to the class.

You can choose a task that suits your intelligence and learning style best, or you can try one that uses another style. By working on an activity that you would not normally choose, you could strengthen another intelligence. Never pass up a challenge – you should always aim to extend yourself as fully as you can.

Visual-linguistic tasks

★ Write a detailed critical appreciation comparing two poems in this challenge. You could use your notes from Activity D and the worksheet entitled 'How to write poetry appreciation' to aid you with this task. Display your work for feedback from other students.

✦ Write a poem about a rite or ritual in your culture. You could speak from the standpoint of someone who questions the validity of the rite or who shows empathy with a person or creature that suffers during it. Alternatively, you could write a celebratory poem. Present your poem to the class and explain what it means. Be prepared to field questions afterwards.

Visual-spatial tasks

★ Create an informative display of the three poems studied in this challenge. Alternatively you could work on rites and rituals in other poems recommended by your teacher. Enlarge the poems on A3 and annotate them so that younger pupils can easily explore their meanings and cultural origins. Add colours, shapes and symbols to bring your work to life. Give a brief presentation to your classmates to explain your display.

✦ Paint or draw the story of one of the poems. Try to bring out the images of the rites and rituals as well as the feelings of the people involved. Try also to reveal the cultural context of your poem. Afterwards, display your picture to the class and explain how you tried to represent the rites and rituals, feelings, images and cultural context. Be prepared to field questions.

Auditory tasks

✦ Memorise one of the poems in this challenge and perform it in front of the class. (You can find tips on how to do this in *The development of the sonnet*, pages 82–84.) In your performance, try to bring out the narrator's feelings, the importance of the rites and rituals, the poetic technique and the cultural context of the poem. You can choose another poem on this theme recommended by your teacher if you wish, but remember that you will need to study it first.

✦ Compose a song or a piece of music that embodies the ideas, feelings and attitudes in one of the poems on rites and rituals. Perform your composition to the class and explain what you tried to do.

Kinaesthetic tasks

✦ Get together with like-minded students and mime the action of one of the poems while a classmate reads it to the class. You could play the role of one of the narrators. Try to show the narrator's feelings as well as the mood and the importance of rites and rituals in your performance. A classmate could videotape your performance to enable you to evaluate your work afterwards.

✦ Rewrite the poem as a mini play and then perform it to the class. Bring out the narrator's feelings, the rites and rituals, the strong images, the cultural context and any other ideas that you think are significant in the poem.

evaluation

 2 Spend some time discussing other students' contributions as well as getting feedback for your own. Share ideas and point out where improvements could be made. Your classmates' feedback will be useful for evaluating your work on this task and for considering your success on the assignment as a whole.

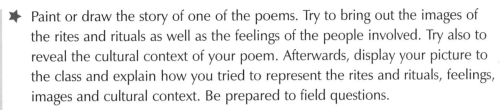

F *Learning review* **20 minutes**

evaluation

 WS 21 1 Fill in the assessment grid and add it to the notes and work from this assignment that you already have in your portfolio.

How confident are you that you achieved the aims of this challenge?

Aim achieved	Not very confident	Reasonably confident	Confident	Very confident
I developed my skills of poetry appreciation.				
I examined how poets from different cultures approached the same theme.				
I made a detailed comparison of two modern poems.				
I produced a creative or analytical piece of work on rites and rituals.				

Next steps

Examine another theme found in modern poetry written in English but from different cultures. For example, you could study the representation of parental figures. Some appropriate poems for this theme would be:

★ 'Poem At Thirty-Nine' by Alice Walker

★ 'Follower' by Seamus Heaney

★ 'Illuminations I' by Tony Harrison.

Or you can select other poems on this or another theme suggested by your teacher.

Target

This challenge will enable you to:

★ identify the stylistic conventions of the following genres of non-fiction texts:
information
recount
explanation
instruction
persuasion
discursive

★ recognise and explain the differences in convention between several types of non-fiction texts

★ use your knowledge by writing an information text that demonstrates the main conventions of non-fiction texts.

About this assignment

This assignment links to other subjects in the curriculum. Your work may incorporate:

★ Design and Technology
★ history
★ geography
★ ICT
★ media
★ music
★ science

Learning styles

For each activity, consider how you might work in the learning style that suits you best:

★ auditory ★ kinaesthetic ★ visual ★ any combination of these.

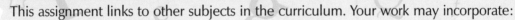

A *Explore the range of non-fiction texts*

30 minutes

knowledge

1 Look at the list of non-fiction text types on the next page. Spend 5 to 10 minutes categorising this list under the activity's main headings. Your teacher may give you a worksheet to save time drawing the table. Some have been entered here to get you started.

Some texts may be listed under more than one heading. Visual-spatial learners may prefer to produce their answers in spidergram or mind map form.

Types of non-fiction texts

health leaflets, diaries, essays, textbooks, manuals, charity leaflets, encyclopaedia entries, autobiography and other accounts of first hand experiences, biography, school reports, field trip reports, recipes, travel guides, travelogues, manifestos, personal letters, letters to newspapers giving opinions, film reviews, statistical reports, advertisements, newspaper editorials, surveys, operating instructions, rules for playing games, briefs, transcripts of court cases, e-mails

The main genres of non-fiction texts

Discursive	Explanation	Information	Instruction	Persuasion	Recount
Essays	Textbooks	Health leaflets	Manuals	Leaflets from charities	Diaries

Information

Definitions

★ Discursive writing can be digressive, wandering on any topic.
★ Recount writing can be anything that is narrated in detail.

synthesis

2 Spend around 10 minutes comparing your notes and add to your table any types of non-fiction texts that you had not thought of so far.

analysis

 1 Read and examine the following four texts as thoroughly as you can. Identify the genre of non-fiction text in each case and make notes as you consider the differences between them.

Text 1

The pace of desert life is almost exactly the opposite of life I'm used to back home. Because of the ferocity of the climate, even the most simple activities must be taken slowly. There is no need to hurry and no benefit in doing so.

For the cameleers, the day follows a timeless, preordained pattern. Prayer, then breakfast cooked over a fire of sticks and branches, then the thick woollen blankets, under which they sleep at night (they don't have tents), are rolled up, secured with twine and laid beside each camel. The camels are brought to their knees and loaded up. Guide ropes are reinserted in mouths stained yellowy-green from cud-chewing, and they are brought to their feet. This provokes a tumult of braying and grunting. I wish I knew what they were saying, for it sounds important to them. Is it passionate protest or is it merely an assertion of team spirit at the start of a new day? Is it 'how many more times do I have to tell you, I'm *not* a beast of burden, right', or is it 'Good morning everyone. Another scorcher by the looks of things'?

Ekawik doesn't speak to me at all. In fact, he doesn't seem the slightest bit interested in making friends with me, despite my sycophantic patting of his flanks and complimentary remarks about the two silver good luck charms hanging from a chain around his neck.

He does, however, honk savagely when asked to carry me. This doesn't help, as I've never felt very comfortable on a ship of the desert. Once perched on Ekawik's hump, I feel about as steady as I would on a surfboard. I've also been provided with a lethal, though aesthetically pleasing, ceremonial saddle with high, spiky prongs and pommels back and front. I may look like some visiting potentate when I'm up there, but when it comes to dismounting, I find it impossible to get my leg over, as it were, and I have to be dragged from the saddle like someone being pulled from a car wreck. Much giggling from the cameleers.

The rhythm of the journey is set by the camels. Normally, they would be on the move at four in the morning, walking for fourteen or fifteen hours a day with two breaks, at midday and late afternoon. Omar tells me that when he's on the road he only has three or four hours' sleep a night.

Ekawik and his friends are happiest when performing something steady, simple and repetitive, like walking or chewing the cud. They are superbly adapted to this climate and terrain. Long legs raise them clear of the hot sand, a layer of fat on their backs protects them from the blazing sun. Heat escapes from their big, reassuringly rounded flanks, so they appear not to perspire, and even in this frightening heat they can go for days without any water at all. And their metabolism, as I've learnt from playing with their nuggets, is extraordinarily economical.

Izambar Mohammed, one of the nine-strong team of cameleers, is the *chanteur*, the one who sings and chants and makes up songs to pass the time as we go. He warns me about staying too close to the camels, especially their rear ends. Using fluent mime, he points out the ones that are the worst kickers. Somehow it doesn't surprise me that they include Ekawik.

From *Sahara* by Michael Palin

Text 2

QUICK BALTI SAUCE

This recipe will not have the depth of flavour of the previous one, but there may be occasions when you have no Balti sauce to hand for use in a recipe and no time to make the full version. You may find the quick sauce a little runnier but to compensate you can adjust the amount of water that you add to the recipe in which you are using this. If you need an even quicker version, replace all the spices with 15 ml (1 tbspn) of Balti spice mix (see page 53) if you have some prepared.

MAKES: ABOUT 570 ML (1 PT)
PREPARATION TIME: 30 MINUTES

45 ml (3 tbspn) ghee or vegetable oil

2 onions, finely chopped

1 clove garlic, crushed

5 ml (1 tspn) paprika

5 ml (1 tspn) ground coriander

2.5 ml (1/2 tspn) ground cumin

Generous pinch of each of salt, chilli powder and ground ginger

400 g (14 oz) can chopped tomatoes in natural juice

1 Heat the ghee or oil in a Balti pan, wok or saucepan over a medium to high heat. Add the onions and garlic and sizzle for about 10 minutes, stirring from time to time, until soft and golden brown.

2 Add the spices and salt and cook, stirring, for 2 minutes.

3 Add the tomatoes, with their juice, and bring to the boil. Simmer for 15 minutes, stirring occasionally.

4 Liquidise the sauce in a food processor or liquidiser, or push through a sieve.

From *Balti: The Complete Cookbook* by Lynette Baxter

Royal Society for the Prevention of Cruelty to Animals

Patron HM The Queen   *Vice Patron* His Grace The Archbishop of Canterbury

Registered charity no. 219099

Will you give an animal the chance this kitten never had?

September 2002

Dear Friend,

This kitten looks so peaceful, she could be dreaming – perhaps of a future filled with good things. Chasing butterflies through the grass…curling up by the fireside…rolling over to have her tummy tickled…learning to love and be loved by a special companion.

But she'll never know how sweet life can be.

At 4 weeks old she was thrown against a wall with such force that she suffered severe head injuries and bones broken in her neck. She died soon afterwards.

If this story angers or saddens you – as it does me – then I would like you to consider supporting the RSPCA with a regular gift of £3 a month to help us stop other animals from suffering similar fates.

When I spoke to Inspector Anthony Pritchard, the RSPCA Inspector who dealt with this case, he said, "This was a savage attack on a defenceless kitten. There's never any excuse for such mindless violence and it sickens me to think of how this animal was abused."

RSPCA Headquarters, Wilberforce Way, Oakhurst Business Park, Southwater, Horsham, West Sussex RH13 9RS
Tel 0870 0101 181 Fax 0870 7530 048 DX 57628 HORSHAM 6 Website: http://www.rspca.org.uk

I am continually impressed by the marvellous people who work at the sharp end for us at the RSPCA, the Inspectors, Animal Collection Officers, Veterinary staff – all of them are totally committed to making the world a better place for the animals we share it with.

But with that commitment comes understandable frustration when they arrive too late, or are unable to save the life of an innocent creature which quite often has suffered unspeakable pain through the ignorance, or in some cases, deliberate cruelty of its owner.

They will ask themselves, would it have been different if we had had more Inspectors, more animal ambulances, better facilities? Because there will always be more that we could have done – but we need your help. We receive no grants or funding from the government for our work. We rely on donations from people like you.

Would you consider starting a regular monthly gift to the RSPCA of £3 a month? Let me tell you why:

Last year the RSPCA's national cruelty and advice line answered 1,509,317 calls from people worried that animals might be suffering or in need of care. Our 328 Inspectors were involved in nearly 12,000 rescues and our team of 146 Animal Collection Officers, working closely with their local Inspectors, collected and transported an astonishing 184,706 animals. We also treated and found new, loving homes for 90,689 animals.

We are also determined that those people who think that it is acceptable to inflict deliberate cruelty on defenceless, vulnerable animals are taught a lesson.

A life snuffed out

This four week-old kitten was thrown against a wall with such force that she suffered severe head injuries and broken bones in her neck. She died soon afterwards. It's too late for her, but many more animals are living in desperate need of your protection. Pets who are starving, beaten, terrified…who've never known a human to touch them in kindness. But you can help us give them a future that for now they can only dream of.

£3 a month will help us protect suffering animals and prosecute cruel owners.

Be a **friend for life**

At five weeks old – too young even to be separated from their mother – tiny kittens Iggy and Pop were ruthlessly dumped in a box by the side of the road on a bitterly cold night. One of our inspectors took them to the local RSPCA Animal Centre. Iggy and Pop were immediately give a health check by Centre staff and, after being treated, they were found loving, responsible owners.

£3 a month will help find a loving new home for unwanted and mistreated animals.

Photo copyright RSPCA photo library.

Text 4

Modern mime.

mime [mim] *noun* (plural mimes)

1. acting using only gesture and action: a style of performance in which people act out situations or portray characters using only gesture and action (often used before a noun)
2. performer who uses mime: a performer who relies on gesture, facial expression, and action rather than using the voice. Also called mime artist
3. theatrical performance in mime: a theatrical piece performed with gesture, facial expression, and action rather than with words
4. ancient farce: in ancient Greek and Roman theatre, a lewd comedy including dialogue, dance, and gesture.

Encarta® World English Dictionary © & (P) 1999 Microsoft Corporation. All rights reserved. Developed for Microsoft by Bloomsbury Publishing plc

2 You are going to consider the conventions used in these four non-fiction texts.

First use the Information box on the next page to help you make a list of the conventions (customary practices) used in non-fiction texts. Use a dictionary to look up any terms that you are unsure about.

Then decide which conventions are used by each text. Notice how some conventions are frequently present in certain types of non-fiction text and completely absent in others. Decide how you will record and present your research. Visual-spatial learners, for example, may like to produce two posters with copies of the texts. The texts could be annotated with the conventions and arrows pointing to particular parts of texts. These posters could be used afterwards for an information display for students at Key Stage 3.

Information

Here are some of the main conventions found in non-fiction texts. However, this list is not exhaustive. You can add other conventions as you discover them.

Person and tense

★ first person – used in autobiography, travel writing

★ present tense – gives a sense of immediacy

★ past tense – can sound more formal, objective

★ third person – used in biography, recount

★ second person, *dear friend*, *you*, etc.

★ third person generic (e.g. kittens, not Iggy the kitten).

Sentence types

★ passive sentences – used for variation or to give a different emphasis. For example, in the RSPCA's leaflet on abandoned kittens, the writer could have used the active sentence: 'Centre staff immediately gave Iggy and Pop a health check …' But the writer instead chooses the passive: 'Iggy and Pop were immediately given a health check by Centre staff …' The passive sentence emphasises the helplessness of the kittens – what was done for them by the RSPCA. The passive voice is sometimes used for less relevant information.

★ short sentences – used for instructions, for emphasis, for clarity, etc.

★ imperative sentences – used for instructions

★ direct speech, quotations and reported speech – used for a variety of reasons; they can add interest, immediacy and veracity

★ rhetorical questions – used to engage the reader.

Linking

★ connectives – used to emphasise cause and effect, sequences, comparisons and logic, for example *then*, *similarly*, *because*, *on the other hand*, *therefore*, etc.

★ phrases to introduce evidence

★ concluding phrases

★ subheadings

★ paragraph openings – help to sequence information in the text such as events, cause and effect, comparison, contrast and adding information.

Punctuation

★ skilful use of punctuation for effect, for example colons, semicolons, dashes

★ limited or simple use of punctuation, for example full stops and commas only.

Presentational devices

★ varied sizes and styles of fonts including fonts associated with particular genres of non-fiction text

★ type styling – bold, underlining, etc.

★ logos

★ handwriting

★ bullet points

★ images for purpose or effect, for example to inform, persuade, explain or advise

★ colour

★ graphical aids such as maps, tables, boxes or diagrams

★ captions for images.

evaluation

 3 Compare your analysis with one or two other pairs and amend or add to your lists as necessary. Do you think it is possible to identify a particular type of non-fiction text by the conventions that are used in it?

There may be a brief whole-class discussion to check everyone's progress. If you contribute to the discussion try to support your points with examples from the texts that you studied.

An in-depth analysis of four non-fiction texts

2–3 hours

1 You are now ready to do an in-depth analysis and comparison of the four sample texts. Work through the text, sentence and word-level questions for each of the four texts. You do not have to answer every question, but for each question that you answer, make sure you answer it for all four texts. You should also include some work at each level.

Work in the way that suits you best. You could arrange your answers as four separate sets of formal notes, using each text's title as a heading. Visual-spatial learners may prefer to present their answers in table form on A2 sized paper or to produce four spidergrams. Auditory learners should read texts aloud as this will help them think through their ideas.

Text level

★ Identify the genre and purpose of the text.

★ Identify its target audience by explaining who would read it.

★ Write a brief summary of the main conventions used in the text.

★ What do you already know about this type of text?

★ What are readers expected to do after reading this text?

★ Say whether you enjoyed reading the text and give reasons for your answer.

★ What kinds of non-fiction texts do you prefer reading in your own time?

Sentence level

★ What are the main presentational devices used in the text's layout?

★ Does the text use imagery (e.g. metaphors and similes) and if so, how does it relate to the text's purpose?

★ What kind of narrative voice is used in the text and why is it appropriate?

★ What kinds of language patterns or structures can you identify in the texts? For example, are the sentences mainly statements, instructions, questions or exclamations? Does one kind of sentence predominate over other types and why?

★ What is the average sentence length and how does this relate to the writer's purpose?

✱ Identify the tone of voice, for example is it reflective, respectful, reassuring, humorous, objective or academic?

Word level

✱ Identify any other special use of language in the text and explain why you think it is used. For example, you could look out for alliteration, emotive language (words and phrases intended to move you to sympathy, pity, etc.), or informal language.

✱ Overall, is the language complex or straightforward? Why is it expressed in this way?

✱ Select a few words from each text that reveal its intended audience.

✱ Does the text contain any humour? If so, give examples of humorous words, phrases, irony or puns and explain why they are used.

✱ Point out any unusual uses of language and explain what this adds to the text's purpose and meaning.

✱ Does the vocabulary of the text remain consistent, or does it change in some way? If so, why?

✱ Does the text use statistics and figures? If so, how do they relate to the text's purpose?

synthesis

 2 Spend some time looking over your notes and think about the differences between each type of non-fiction text.

evaluation

 3 In a whole-class discussion, focus on the differences between the four texts and agree on some conventions that could be considered characteristic of these non-fiction text types. During the discussion, consider any interesting differences in interpretation or new points raised by other students. Make a note of anything that you think is important or significant for identifying and distinguishing non-fiction texts.

 E *Produce a non-fiction text* 2–3 hours

application

 1 Your task is to produce an information text that demonstrates your knowledge of the various genres of non-fiction texts and the similarities or differences between them. Choose the activity that suits your strongest intelligence or learning style.

If you want to work in a pair, then team up with someone who is interested in the same task. Your audience will be members of the class and other students in Key Stage 3

Remember to draw on all the work you have done so far in this challenge, using all your knowledge of non-fiction conventions as you plan and produce your own non-fiction text.

★ Produce an A2 poster on non-fiction texts, showing how to spot the main conventions of each text type. Display your poster and talk your audience through its main points.

★ Make a video with brief extracts of non-fiction texts read aloud. Include an 'expert' commentary on the texts' conventions and the way they can vary in different text types.

★ Write an encyclopaedia entry detailing the conventions of non-fiction texts and the differences between types.

★ Write a talk about two or three non-fiction texts of your choice. As part of the talk, include OHTs which the presenter can use to point to and annotate parts of text as they speak. Ensure the talk covers the ways in which each text's conventions differs from others.

★ Design a website in which three or more examples of non-fiction texts are cited and their conventions explained through the use of interactive features. Include a table or some other device to give a brief summary of the differing usage of conventions in the texts.

★ Plan and record a talk about non-fiction texts and their conventions that could be used as a teaching resource for younger students.

★ Produce a clip or loose-leaf folder with two examples of each type of non-fiction text. Organise the texts by their conventions and place summary sheets at the beginning of each section to show the main conventions used in each type of text. Include a table that gives an overview of the conventions of different types of non-fiction texts.

evaluation

 2 Review your work individually and as a class. Did you agree with everyone's ideas and interpretations on non-fiction texts? Make a note of any points or unresolved issues that you would like to follow up by doing further research.

evaluation

1 Fill in the assessment grid and add it to the notes and work from this assignment that you already have in your portfolio.

How confident are you that you achieved the aims of this challenge?

Aim achieved	Not very confident	Reasonably confident	Confident	Very confident
I can identify the main stylistic conventions of non-fiction texts.				
I am aware of the conventions typically used in several types of non-fiction texts.				
I demonstrated my understanding by creating and presenting a non-fiction text.				

Next steps

Find out how the conventions of fiction texts differ from those for non-fiction texts. Carry out a survey, then draw up a table and list the main conventions under two headings: 'Fiction texts' and 'Non-fiction texts'.

Target

This challenge will enable you to:

* compare the parallel worlds created by the authors of:
  Harry Potter and the Philosopher's Stone
  Artemis Fowl
  A Wizard of Earthsea

* consider how each novel fits within the action–adventure genre

* identify similarities and differences between 'heroes' of each novel

* appreciate similarities and differences between the written style of the three novels.

About this assignment

This assignment links to other subjects in the curriculum. Your work may incorporate:

* art and design
* ICT
* media

Learning styles

For each activity, consider how you might work in the learning style that suits you best:

* auditory
* kinaesthetic
* visual
* any combination of these.

A — The narrative structure of action–adventure novels

20 minutes

All three novels belong to the magical–fantasy genre, which is a sub-genre of action–adventure. The narrative in each novel is constructed around the central character – who is usually a hero. The genre also includes stories of comic-book heroes such as Batman, Superman and Spider-Man.

knowledge

1 Work out the narrative structure of an action–adventure novel or film that you have either read or seen. The best way of doing this is to trace the development of the hero within the text's narrative. Produce a summary of what happens to

the hero during the course of the story, either in linear form with headings, or as a flowchart or spidergram (with or without images).

2 Spend 5 minutes or so checking your work before taking part in a whole-class discussion. Decide which of you will offer your feedback.

 B *Compare three magical–fantasy texts* 2–3 hours

knowledge

1 Read the following extracts from three well-known novels in the magical–fantasy subgenre of the action–adventure genre. You should read each one at least twice.

Text 1

Having discovered that he is in fact a wizard, Harry Potter excitedly leaves the world of the 'muggles' (non-wizards) to fulfil his destiny by enrolling at Hogwarts, a school for wizards. But first he needs to find the right platform so he can catch his train.

Harry woke at five o'clock the next morning and was too excited and nervous to go back to sleep. He got up and pulled on his jeans because he didn't want to walk into the station in his wizard's robes – he'd change on the train. He checked his Hogwarts list yet again to make sure he had everything he needed, saw that Hedwig was shut safely in her cage and then paced the room, waiting for the Dursleys to get up. Two hours later, Harry's huge, heavy trunk had been loaded into the Dursleys' car, Aunt Petunia had talked Dudley into sitting next to Harry and they had set off.

They reached King's Cross at half past ten. Uncle Vernon dumped Harry's trunk on to a trolley and wheeled it into the station for him. Harry thought this was strangely kind until Uncle Vernon stopped dead, facing the platforms with a nasty grin on his face.

'Well, there you are, boy. Platform nine – platform ten. Your platform should be somewhere in the middle, but they don't seem to have built it yet, do they?'

He was quite right, of course. There was a big plastic number nine over one platform and a big plastic number ten over the one next to it, and in the middle, nothing at all

'Have a good term,' said Uncle Vernon with an even nastier smile. He left without another word. Harry turned and saw the Dursleys drive away. All three of them were laughing. Harry's mouth went rather dry. What on earth was he going to do? He was starting to attract lots of funny looks, because of Hedwig. He'd have to ask someone.

He stopped a passing guard, but didn't dare mention platform nine and three-quarters. The guard had never heard of Hogwarts and when Harry couldn't even tell him what part of the country it was in, he started to get annoyed, as though Harry was being stupid on purpose. Getting desperate, Harry asked for the train that left at eleven o'clock, but the guard said there wasn't one. In the end the guard strode away, muttering about time-wasters. Harry was now trying hard not to panic. According to the large clock over the arrivals board, he had ten minutes left to get on the train to Hogwarts and he had no idea how to do it; he was stranded in the middle of a station with a trunk he could hardly lift, a pocket full of wizard money and a large owl.

Hagrid must have forgotten to tell him something you had to do, like tapping the third brick on the left to get into Diagon Alley. He wondered if he should get out his wand and start tapping the ticket box between platforms nine and ten.

At that moment a group of people passed just behind him and he caught a few words of what they were saying.

'– packed with Muggles, of course –'

Harry swung round. The speaker was a plump woman who was talking to four boys, all with flaming red hair. Each of them was pushing a trunk like Harry's in front of him – and they had an *owl*.

Heart hammering, Harry pushed his trolley after them. They stopped and so did he, just near enough to hear what they were saying.

'Now, what's the platform number?' said the boys' mother.

'Nine and three-quarters!' piped a small girl, also red-headed, who was holding her hand. 'Mum, can't I go …'

'You're not old enough, Ginny, now be quiet. All right, Percy, you go first.'

What looked like the oldest boy marched towards platforms nine and ten. Harry watched, careful not to blink in case he missed it – but just as the boy reached the divide between the two platforms, a large crowd of tourists came swarming in front of him, and by the time the last rucksack had cleared away, the boy had vanished.

'Fred, you next,' the plump woman said.

'I'm not Fred, I'm George,' said the boy. 'Honestly, woman, call yourself our mother? Can't you *tell* I'm George?'

'Sorry, George, dear.'

'Only joking, I am Fred,' said the boy, and off he went. His twin called after him to hurry up, and he must have done, because a second later, he had gone – but how had he done it?

Now the third brother was walking briskly towards the ticket barrier – he was almost there – and then, quite suddenly, he wasn't anywhere.

There was nothing else for it.

'Excuse me,' Harry said to the plump woman.

'Hullo, dear,' she said. 'First time at Hogwarts? Ron's new, too.'

She pointed at the last and youngest of her sons. He was tall, thin and gangling, with freckles, big hands and feet and a long nose.

'Yes,' said Harry. 'The thing is – the thing is, I don't know how to – '

'How to get on to the platform?' she said kindly, and Harry nodded.

'Not to worry,' she said. 'All you have to do is walk straight at the barrier between platforms nine and ten. Don't stop and don't be scared you'll crash into it, that's very important. Best do it at a bit of a run if you're nervous. Go on, go now before Ron.'

'Er – OK', said Harry.

He pushed his trolley round and stared at the barrier. It looked very solid.

He started to walk towards it. People jostled him on their way to platforms nine and ten. Harry walked more quickly. He was going to smash right into that ticket box and then he'd be in trouble – leaning forward on his trolley he broke into a heavy run – the barrier was coming nearer and nearer – he wouldn't be able to stop – the trolley was out of control – he was a foot away – he closed his eyes ready for the crash –

It didn't come … he kept on running … he opened his eyes.

A scarlet steam engine was waiting next to a platform packed with people. A sign overhead said *Hogwarts Express, 11 o'clock*. Harry looked behind him and saw a wrought-iron archway where the ticket box had been, with the words *Platform Nine and Three-Quarters* on it. He had done it.

From *Harry Potter and the Philosopher's Stone* by J. K. Rowling

Text 2

The story, which is set in a mythical past, is centred on a motherless young boy known as Sparrowhawk, who later learns that his real name is Ged. He is sent by Ogion, his mentor, to the School for Wizards on the island of Roke to broaden his knowledge of magic.

Ged slept that night aboard *Shadow*, and early in the morning parted with those first sea-comrades of his, they shouting good wishes cheerily after him as he went up the docks. The town of Thwil is not large, its high houses huddling close over a few steep narrow streets. To Ged, however, it seemed a city, and not knowing where to go he asked the first townsman of Thwil he met where he would find the Warder of the School on Roke. The man looked at him sidelong a while and said, 'The wise don't need to ask, the fool asks in vain,' and so went on along the street. Ged went uphill till he came out into a square, rimmed on three sides by the houses with their sharp slate roofs and on the fourth side by the wall of a great building whose few small windows were higher than the chimney tops of the houses: a fort or castle it seemed, built of mighty grey blocks of stone. In the square beneath it market-booths were set up and there was some coming and going of people. Ged asked his question of an old woman with a basket of mussels, and she replied, 'You cannot always find the Warder where he is, but sometimes you find him where he is not,' and went on crying her mussels to sell.

In the great building, near one corner, there was a mean little door of wood. Ged went to this and knocked loud. To the old man who opened the door he said, 'I bear a letter from the Mage Ogion of Gont to the Warder of the School on this island. I want to find the Warder, but I will not hear more riddles and scoffing!'

'This is the School,' the old man said mildly. 'I am the doorkeeper. Enter if you can.'

Ged stepped forward. It seemed to him that he had passed through the doorway: yet he stood outside on the pavement where he had stood before.

Once more he stepped forward, and once more he remained standing outside the door. The doorkeeper, inside, watched him with mild eyes.

Ged was not so much baffled as angry, for this seemed like a further mockery to him. With voice and hand he made the Opening spell which his aunt had taught him long ago; it was the prize among all her stock of spells, and he wove it well now. But it was only a witch's charm, and the power that held this doorway was not moved at all.

When that failed Ged stood a long while there on the pavement. At last he looked at the old man who waited inside. 'I cannot enter,' he said unwillingly, 'unless you help me.'

The doorkeeper answered, 'Say your name.'

Then again Ged stood still a while; for a man never speaks his own name aloud, until more than his life's safety is at stake.

'I am Ged,' he said aloud. Stepping forward then he entered the open doorway. Yet it seemed to him that though the light was behind him, a shadow followed him at his heels.

He saw also as he turned that the doorway through which he had come was not plain wood as he had thought, but ivory without joint or seam: it was cut, as he knew later, from a tooth of the Great Dragon. The door that the old man closed behind him was of polished horn, through which the daylight shone dimly, and on its inner face was carved the Thousand-Leaved Tree.

'Welcome to this house, lad,' the doorkeeper said, and without saying more led him through halls and corridors to an open court far inside the walls of the building. The court was partly paved with stone, but was roofless, and on a grass-plot a fountain played under young trees in the sunlight. There Ged waited alone some while. He stood still, and his heart beat hard, for it seemed to him that he felt presences and powers at work unseen about him here, and he knew that this place was built not only of stone but of magic stronger than stone. He stood in the innermost room of the House of the Wise, and it was open to the sky. Then suddenly he was aware of a man clothed in white who watched him through the falling water of the fountain.

As their eyes met, a bird sang aloud in the branches of the tree. In that moment Ged understood the singing of the bird, and the language of the

water falling in the basin of the fountain, and the shape of the clouds, and the beginning and end of the wind that stirred the leaves: it seemed to him that he himself was a word spoken by the sunlight.

From *A Wizard of Earthsea* by Ursula Le Guin

Text 3

Twelve-year-old Artemis Fowl, an ingenious criminal mastermind, has searched the world with his powerful manservant, Butler, for *The Book*. He believes that *The Book*'s magical secrets will bring him gold and raise his family's fortunes once again. Nguyen, a shady contact made on the Internet, leads Artemis to one of *The People*, an alcoholic sprite living in Ho Chi Minh City. Artemis tricks the sprite into letting him look at her copy of *The Book* for 30 of his 'human minutes'. She thinks that a 'mud' person like Artemis will never be able to understand its script. However, Artemis secretly uses his technological know-how to photograph *The Book* digitally and download its contents to Fowl Manor in Dublin. In this extract, Artemis has just returned home and is trying to decipher *The Book*.

The Book was proving far more stubborn than Artemis had anticipated. It seemed to be almost actively resisting him. No matter which program he ran it through, the computer came up blank.

Artemis hard-copied every page, tacking them to the walls of his study. Sometimes it helped to have things on paper. The script was like nothing he'd seen before, and yet it was strangely familiar. Obviously a mixture of symbolic and character-based language, the text meandered around the page in no apparent order.

What the program needed was some frame of reference, some central point on which to build. He separated all the characters and ran comparisons with English, Chinese, Greek, Arabic and Cyrillic texts, even with Ogham. Nothing.

Moody with frustration, Artemis sent Juliet scurrying when she interrupted with sandwiches, and moved on to symbols. The most frequently recurring pictogram was a small male figure. Male, he presumed, though with the limited knowledge of the fairy anatomy he supposed it could be female.

A thought struck him. Artemis opened the ancient languages file on his Power Translator and selected Egyptian.

At last. A hit. The male symbol was remarkably similar to the Anubis god representation on Tutankhamen's inner-chamber hieroglyphics. This was consistent with his other findings. The first written human stories were about fairies, suggesting that their civilization predated man's own. It would seem that the Egyptians had simply adapted an existing scripture to suit their needs.

There were other resemblances. But the characters were just dissimilar enough to slip through the computer's net. This would have to be done manually. Each Gnommish figure had to be enlarged, printed and then compared with the hieroglyphs.

Artemis felt the excitement of success thumping inside his ribcage. Almost every fairy pictogram or letter had an Egyptian counterpart. Most were universal, such as the sun or birds. But some seemed exclusively supernatural and had to be tailored to fit. The Anubis figure, for example, would make no sense as a dog god, so Artemis altered it to read king of the fairies.

By midnight, Artemis had successfully fed his findings into the Macintosh. All he had to do now was press 'Decode'. He did so. What emerged was a long, intricate string of meaningless gibberish.

A normal child would have abandoned the task long since. The average adult would probably have been reduced to slapping the keyboard. But not Artemis. This book was testing him and he would not allow it to win.

The letters were right, he was certain of it. It was just the order that was wrong. Rubbing the sleep from his eyes, Artemis glared at the pages again. Each segment was bordered by a solid line. This could represent paragraphs or chapters, but they were not meant to be read in the usual left to right, top to bottom fashion.

Artemis experimented. He tried the Arabic right to left and the Chinese columns. Nothing worked. Then he noticed that each page had one thing in common – a central section. The other pictograms were arranged around this pivotal area. So a central starting point perhaps. But where to go from there? Artemis scanned the pages for some other common factor. After several minutes he found it. There was on each page a tiny spearhead in the corner of one section. Could this be an arrow? A direction? Go this way?

So the theory would be start in the middle, then follow the arrow, reading in spirals.

The computer program wasn't built to handle something like this, so Artemis had to improvise. With a craft knife and ruler, he dissected the first page of the Book and reassembled it in the traditional Western languages order – left to right, parallel rows. Then he rescanned the page and fed it through the modified Egyptian translator:

The computer hummed and whirred, converting all the information to binary. Several times it stopped to ask for confirmation of a character or symbol. This happened less and less as the machine learned the new language. Eventually two words flashed on the screen: **File converted**.

Fingers shaking from exhaustion and excitement, Artemis clicked 'Print'. A single page scrolled from the LaserWriter. It was in English now. Yes, there were mistakes, some fine-tuning needed, but it was perfectly legible and, more importantly, perfectly understandable.

Fully aware that he was probably the first human in several thousand years to decode the magical words, Artemis switched on his desk light and began to read.

The Booke of the People.
Being instructions to our magicks and life rules

Carry me always, carry me well.
I am thy teacher of herb and spell.
I am thy link to power arcane.
Forget me and thy magick shall wane.

Ten times ten commandments there be.
They will answer every mystery.
Cures, curses, alchemy.
These secrets shall be thine, through me.

But, Fairy, remember this above all.
I am not for those in mud that crawl.
And forever doomed shall be the one,
Who betrays my secrets one by one.

Artemis could hear the blood pumping in his ears. He had them. They would be as ants beneath his feet. Their every secret would be laid bare by technology. Suddenly the exhaustion claimed him and he sank back in his chair. There was so much yet to complete. Forty-three pages to be translated for a start.

He pressed the intercom button that linked him to speakers all over the house. 'Butler. Get Juliet and come up here. There are some jigsaws I need you to assemble.'

From *Artemis Fowl* by Eoin Colfer

analysis

2 With a partner work through these text, sentence and word-level questions that follow, rereading parts of the text as necessary. You do not have to answer every question, but make sure that you include some work at each level. Try to organise your answers in a way that suits your main learning style.

Text level

★ Briefly sum up what each extract is about and explain how they are related to each other.

★ What kind of parallel world has been constructed in each text?

★ What are your views of the main characters?

★ What are their relationships like with other characters?

★ In what ways are the main characters the same or different from one another?

★ How does each text fit within the sub-genre of magical–fantasy?

★ If you have not read any of these three books, describe how you expect their plots will unfold.

Sentence level

★ Think about the tone of voice of each third-person narrator. Place the narrators in order from the lightest to the darkest in tone. Then explain your order using brief quotations from the text.

★ Which extract has the most suspense? Give reasons for your choice.

★ Describe the images, language and layout that each writer uses to help their audience imagine the scene.

★ Which extract did you most enjoy reading? Give reasons for your answer.

Word level

★ Which text uses the most challenging vocabulary? Give one or two examples to support your choice.

★ Identify the text in which names and the words used for things matter most; explain why you think this is so.

★ Some readers of *Artemis Fowl* claim to be able to decipher the Gnomish script in the novel. Can you translate the Gnomish script at the bottom of the extract here? (If you decide to try, you could look at the website, detailed in the Resources box, which offers support, advice and encouragement.)

★ Is it possible to establish the intended audience for each text from its vocabulary? Again give at least one reason for your answer.

Resources 1

Excellent information and advice on each of the three novels can be found at Reading Matters.
http://www.readingmatters.co.uk/index.htm

Artemis Fowl Fun is definitely worth a visit too.
http://artemisfowl.tripod.com/index.htm

Some of the reviews of *Artemis Fowl* at Amazon Books UK also refer to the Gnomish script and how readers figured it out.

evaluation

 3

Spend a few minutes going over your answers with a partner before discussing them in class. During the class discussion, follow up any interesting points raised by asking more questions and adding any fresh ideas to your notes.

C Read and compare two magical–fantasy novels

 about 20 hours

analysis

 1

Read and compare two or all three novels, and report on their similarities and differences. This activity will be useful for some of the creative activities later on in this challenge. Use the questions below to guide your enquiry. You can, of course, make linear or spidergram notes to record your main ideas.

★ What do you think are the main themes and messages of each novel? (One common theme, for example, is good and evil.)

★ How are the themes of each novel represented in its imagery? For example, the imagery of light and dark in *A Wizard of Earthsea* is linked to the theme of good and evil. (Remember also to look for imagery in the similes, metaphors and personification used).

★ Do the characters change during the course of each novel? If so, how?

★ What do you think are the main similarities and differences between each novel's character, plot, settings and narrative tone (how serious is the voice of each narrator)?

You could draw your main ideas for each text together in a comparison web, like the one below. This will enable you to organise ideas more easily and help you prepare for the class. Simply add boxes as you think of more similarities and differences.

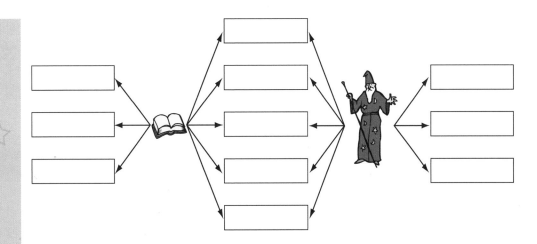

  2 As a class, discuss your comparison of the novels, focusing on the four questions. Add to your notes any fresh and interesting points raised by others. If necessary, revisit relevant parts of the novels to iron out any misreading of the text or to clarify your understanding.

D *Novel presentation of novel ideas*   *1–2 hours*

---

application

  1 Choose one of the tasks below and present your work to the class in the manner that is appropriate for that task.

Visual-linguistic tasks

✦ Write a short chapter in which two or more of the central characters from the novels meet at a school for wizards. What would they say to each other and how would they behave? Use your knowledge of each character's inner life and motivations to help you construct the scene.

✦ Create a series of web pages to help readers understand the genre of the novels and the links that can be made between them. You could also highlight important differences between the novels and give advice about important points to look for in each text. Your target audience could be students in Years 6, 7 and 8.

Visual-spatial tasks

✦ Compare one or more of the novels with its film version. How does the novel translate to the screen? What is left out and what is added?

✦ Examine the book covers for each of the three novels and analyse how the genre, themes and ideas of each are represented in the images, colours, fonts and blurb.

★ Design new book covers for at least two of the novels, reviewing the notes that you made during this assignment for ideas. Ensure each cover reflects the genre as well as showing the main characters and themes. Also consider the audience in each case. Display the original covers alongside your own book and comment on how they compare. Explain also how each of your covers would help to sell the book to its audience.

Resources 2

A Wizard of Earthsea has had a number of different covers over the years. To see them, go to this website created by a fan of Ursula Le Guin. **http://hem.passagen.se/peson42/lgw/sitemap.html**

Click on the title of the novel on the site map. You can enlarge the book covers by clicking on them.

Auditory-task

★ Read over your notes that you made for Activity C and produce a tape that could be used as a teaching resource to help younger students understand significant links between the three novels. Your tape should include information on the novels' genre, characters, themes, similarities and differences, as well as other features that you think are important.

Kinaesthetic tasks

★ Create a board game based on your knowledge of this sub-genre of action–adventure novels. You can, if necessary, adapt the board design and rules of a game that you already know. Your game should be suitable for use as an educational toy to help new young audiences understand the genre, main characters, and links between the novels.

★ Videotape a series of interviews with 'expert' students on the three novels' genre, characters, themes and links. Your main aim should be to help Key Stage 3 students gain a comparative understanding of the novels. You will need to make a decision about whether you will edit out the questions that you put to your experts so that they appear as 'talking heads', giving fairly long answers to silent questions. (Watch interviews on the BBC's Open University to observe the effectiveness of this technique.) Alternatively, you will need someone to act as a link person between the interviews.

evaluation

 2 Review your presentations as a class and talk about what went well and what could have been done better. Think about what you learned through working on

this assignment. Was every activity useful or could some activities be changed to make them more effective?

Make a note of any part of the assignment that you may need to research further to clarify your understanding.

E *Learning review*

15 minutes

1 Fill in the assessment grid and add it to the notes and work that you already have in your portfolio.

How confident are you that you achieved the aims of this challenge?

Aim achieved	Not very confident	Reasonably confident	Confident	Very confident
I was able to compare the parallel worlds in the three novels.				
I was able to work out how the novels fitted within the action–adventure genre.				
I identified some similarities and differences between the 'heroes' of each novel.				
I could appreciate similarities and differences between the written style of the three novels.				

Next steps

Each of the novels studied in this assignment is part of a trilogy or a series. If you have developed a taste for the novels of this genre, why not read the next book in the series? If you have not already read it, you may also like to try the classic trilogy of this genre, J. R. R. Tolkien's *The Lord of the Rings*.

Target

This challenge will enable you to:

★ understand how superheroes are represented in comic books and in films, looking in particular at *Spider-Man*

★ identify how character development and the theme of 'responsibility and power' are represented in *Spider-Man*

★ appreciate how film director Sam Raimi used the following key elements of film language within his *Spider-Man* narrative:
    lighting and colour
    sound
    camera shots and camera movement
    mise en scène
    editing

★ demonstrate your knowledge of film language in a creative task.

About this assignment

This assignment links to other subjects in the curriculum. Your work may incorporate:

★ art   ★ ICT

★ music   ★ RE

Learning styles

For each activity, consider how you might work in the learning style that suits you best:

★ auditory   ★ kinaesthetic   ★ visual   ★ any combination of these.

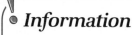

A   *How is Spider-Man represented?*

 2–3 hours

Information

Several comic-book superheroes are modern representations of heroes from fairytale, folklore and Greek myths. Like their forerunners, modern superheroes often have a flaw or point of weakness. The plots of modern superhero stories often embody morals and lessons that are important for young people.

> Unlike directors of some other comic-book hero films, *Spider-Man's*, director, Sam Raimi, stuck with the message implicit in the original comic books published by Marvel: 'with great power, comes great responsibility'. In both comic and film, Peter Parker has to experience the loss of his uncle before he can learn this truth. The film is about exercising the power of choice through responsibility – something everyone needs to learn as they grow up.

knowledge

 1 Watch the film *Spider-Man*. Watch also, if you can, the feature on the second DVD called: *Spider-Man: The Mythology of the 21st Century*.

Then make notes on how you think Spider-Man is represented in comic strips and films. You can do this as linear notes with headings and bullets or as a spidergram.

evaluation

 2 Discuss your notes and ideas in a whole-class session. Ask questions about issues and points that you would like to follow up. Explore any interesting ideas put forward by others.

Here is one idea that you could follow up. The main moral lesson in *Spider-Man* is 'with great power comes great responsibility'. Are there moral messages in other superhero stories, or is *Spider-Man* special in this respect? You could research the question by reading some Marvel comics and by using a good search engine on the Internet.

B Build a superhero profile

 3–4 hours

knowledge

 1 You might be asked to do some of this activity for homework and complete it afterwards with a partner in class.

Extend your knowledge of Spider-Man or another comic-book superhero by building up a profile of the character and the stories. Begin by reading some of the original comic-strip stories. You could read some episodes from the Marvel comic books or you could buy a current comic. The DVD summarises a few episodes from the *Spider-Man* comic series from every decade since the 1960s. Use the questions below to guide your research and make notes in the way that best suits your strongest learning style. You may also find it helpful to look at some of the websites suggested in Resources box 1.

* Are there 'typical' storylines and if so, how would you summarise them?

* Who are the arch-enemies; what are their powers, motives and actions?

* What important messages and ideas are contained in the stories?

* In what ways can Peter Parker (or another superhero) be described as 'ordinary'?

* How are women presented in the stories?

* How are current or topical events presented?

* How do real locations affect the audiences of *Spider-Man*? What kinds of locations are used in other superhero stories and why do you think they were created?

* Identify the target audience for *Spider-Man* (or other superhero) stories and why these people like them particularly.

* Why were these superheroes created in America? Why do you think that they have become popular in other English-speaking cultures including our own?

Resources 1

Here are two websites where you can find a lot of information on Spider-Man. You can also find web links on the *Spider-Man* DVD.

The official movie site
http://www.thespidermanmovie.com/Spider-man-2002/index.html

Good background information can be found on the Action–Adventure Movies website:
http://actionadventure.about.com/cs/spiderman

Here are some essays on the origins of superheroes.

Superherohype
http://www.superherohype.com/spider-man/articles/spiderman.php

'The birth of a superhero'
http://members.lycos.co.uk/TheDraft/Superman_04_Hero.htm

'Man of Steel and Myth: The Need for and Creation of The Superhero' by Elizabeth Miller
http://www.greenfireburning.com/words/superhero.html

evaluation

 2 Share your superhero profile with a partner so you can check each other's findings and discuss your ideas with each other. Then share your ideas in a whole-class discussion. Ask questions on anything that you would like to know more about.

The director did not want to open the film with an action scene. Instead Raimi wanted his audience to see how Peter Parker develops from the nerdy 'boy next door' who lacks social confidence into someone who is thrilled with his new powers, although rather unsure about them.

For each part of this activity, watch the selected scenes as a class before making notes on the questions individually. Your notes do not have to be extensive and can be in linear or spidergram form, to suit your learning style. Then have a 10-minute whole-class session to evaluate your answers.

comprehension

 1 Examine how Peter Parker's character develops in the opening scenes of the film.

✦ Watch the bus and the Columbia University scenes. How is Peter represented here?

✦ Look again at the cafeteria and corridor scenes where Peter becomes aware of new reflexes and 'spidey sense'. How does this affect Peter's character?

✦ Now look at the scene where Peter learns about his powers to climb and jump great distances. Why, for example, is jumping off the roof for the first time such an important experience for him? Explain how Peter changes in these scenes and the effect that the new powers have upon his character.

2 Watch the scene where Peter wants to impress Mary Jane by buying a new car but lacks the money to do so. While reading newspaper adverts for cars he discovers an advert for a wrestling competition, but finds that he has to create a 'colourful character'. For Peter, this becomes an exercise in visual metacognition (thinking about thinking), how does the director represent him doing this? To answer this question you may find it helpful to look at some of the film terms on the website suggested below.

Resources 2

A very good site for finding out about film terms:

'Cinematographical & film production terms'
http://www.theblackbook.net/acad/tagg/teaching/mmi/filmtrms.html#

3 Look again at the scenes from Peter's argument with his uncle in the car to the point where he catches up with his uncle's murderer. Explain what Peter learns and how this relates to his character's development. How could Peter be said to be using metacognition?

4 Compare the backgrounds of Peter and his college friend Harry Osborn. How does Harry cope with wealth and responsibility in his relationships with other characters? In what ways is he different from Peter?

5 After pushing the limits of science too far, Harry's father, Norman Osborn, turns into a modern Jekyll and Hyde character.* How does Norman's attitude to power and responsibility compare with Peter's? Explore this issue after looking at the rooftop scene where the Green Goblin tempts a weakened Spider-Man by offering him a partnership in return for 'power'. Which Bible story does this recall?

evaluation

6 Now draw your ideas together and discuss them as a whole. You will have found that the story ultimately covers good and evil as its main theme. But how do the Osborns and the Parkers compare? Discuss this as a class, considering the following questions.

★ What are each family's attitudes towards power and responsibility?

★ What do they each learn, or fail to learn?

★ What does the audience learn about Peter Parker and Harry Osborn as the film progresses?

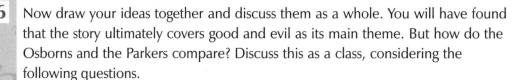

D *Explore film language and convention in* Spider-Man

about 14 hours

This activity focuses on different aspects of film language. In each section, you will first need to study the Information box to acquaint yourself with some basic facts. In some sections you may also want to look at the suggested web sites to research the topic in more depth. Always make sure you have understood the ideas before you move onto the question that follows. If necessary, discuss the ideas in pairs or as a class to check your understanding.

*The idea on which Norman Osborn's character is based comes from a novel by Robert Louis Stevenson called The Strange Case of Dr Jekyll and Mr Hyde. *If you would like to research this link further, you can find Stevenson's text in your library or at a website called* The Literature Network:
http://www.online-literature.com/stevenson/jekyllhyde/

Information

Film language

Just as novels have certain elements and conventions such as characters, themes, mood, atmosphere and imagery, films also use a number of conventions – they have their own 'language'. Some knowledge of these conventions can help you to appreciate a film and to understand how it works. Every film tells a story and the director has the biggest say in how it is put together. You need to remember that films are heavily constructed right down to the smallest detail. Everything that you see and hear must, in some way, help tell the story and contribute to the film's atmosphere or communicate its themes and ideas.

All this may not seem obvious when you are watching the latest blockbuster movie at your local cinema. This is because it is the film director's job to sell you an entertaining piece of fantasy and to get you to go along with the story. In *Spider-Man* this is quite an enormous task given the comic book origins of the story! However, Sam Raimi, the director, does an excellent job – perhaps because he has been a fan of this superhero since childhood.

Resources 3

A Basic Glossary of Film Terms
http://arts.anu.edu.au/arthistory/ht_docs/fs_units/glossary.htm

Glossarist: film glossaries and film dictionaries
http://www.glossarist.com/glossaries/arts-culture/film.asp

Lighting

 1 hour

Information

How lighting helps tell the story
Lighting helps set the mood and atmosphere of a scene. It encourages the audience to interpret what they see in a particular way.

A fully lit scene* creates a bright, non-threatening atmosphere which is a good setting for open and sometimes humorous dialogue between the actors. Consider the scenes where Peter Parker gradually becomes conscious of his powers as he discovers that everything he touches sticks to him. These humorous scenes are not sinister and are therefore fully lit.

Bright lighting on a particular object or a gesture or movement made by an actor can highlight its significance for the plot. For example, think about the scene where Peter's blood falls from his wrist; the splash alerts Norman Osborn to his presence.

Scenes shot at night or with dark shadows often imply something menacing where a character is threatened, injured or worse. Villains in films usually carry out their darkest deeds in the shadows. A partially lit scene full of shadows can create an atmosphere of dread or suspense. For a good example in *Spider-Man*, look again at the scene where Peter Parker only gets paid $100, rather than the $3,000 he had expected. This whole scene, including the robbery, is shot with low lighting and is full of shadows. Notice also that most of the evil deeds of the Green Goblin and other crooks are usually carried out at night.

* Film directors construct films by making scenes, all of which have scene numbers. Each scene has a specific purpose, which might be to do with development of character or plot. Scenes always begin and end in the same location and can last a few seconds or several minutes. However, in today's fast-moving films, the general trend is for shorter scenes.

Lighting on film sets

Directors have no problem getting light; the important thing is to control it in order to create the desired effect. The quality of the light is far more important than the quantity.

There are three main types of light on a film set:

★ key lights – the main source of illumination on a set which determines the general level and pattern of brightness

★ backlights – at the back of the set to add depth or highlights

★ filler lights – to remove any unwanted shadows or contrasts created by the key light.

Sometimes directors use these lights for daylight scenes as well, especially when natural light (called 'available light') is low. Directors often use available light when they want to give their films a realistic, documentary feel.

For filming indoors, directors can create a variety of effects by using:

★ underlighting – this throws out shadows and can create scary effects

- ✦ toplighting – overhead lighting that can highlight features of a character; it can also lend a touch of glamour

- ✦ backlighting – used when key lights and filler lights are switched off. It is used to create effects such as silhouettes and can add to the atmosphere of fear and suspense.

analysis

 1

In pairs, look at two chapters from the *Spider-Man* DVD and compare the way in which the lighting helps to create the mood in each. Make notes in either linear or spidergram form.

By working in a pair, you can divide the points that you want to look or listen out for before each viewing. That way you can cover more ground and then compare your notes and ideas afterwards.

The DVD's chapter titles provide reference points for finding scenes, but remember that chapters can include more than one scene. Try to choose two contrasting scenes to compare. You could, for example, look at scenes from:

- ✦ Chapter 7, Fight with Flash

- ✦ Chapter 11, Enter the thief

- ✦ Chapter 12, The death of Uncle Ben.

evaluation

 2

Talk about your findings in a whole-class discussion. Add to your notes any fresh and interesting points. Take the opportunity to ask questions because someone in the class may well know the answer.

Colour

 20 minutes

Information

Communicating through colour

It was a US company called Technicolor that introduced colour to mainstream films in the early 1930s. The result for audiences was dramatic because directors were able to introduce a whole new range of effects by the use of colour. The biggest impact was, perhaps, in films of fantasy and spectacle such as *The Wizard of Oz* (1939) and *Gone with the Wind* (1939).

Because of *Spider-Man*'s comic book origins, colour was especially important for this film. Notice how the strong use of primary colours produces a comic-book effect. Many of Spider-Man's poses were taken from colourful shots from the comic strip.

The use of colour can reveal a character's feelings and emotions; it can signify themes and ideas; it can set the moods of a scene. The way a director uses colour can even set the tone of the whole film. As *Spider-Man* progresses, the mood becomes darker and this is reflected in the colours used.

knowledge

  3

In pairs, quickly explore what colours can symbolise. On a large sheet of paper, write some different colours as headings, then brainstorm the meanings that can be symbolically associated with each one. For example, green has several symbolic meanings including jealousy, life and growth.

evaluation

  4

Form groups of four and compare your ideas with another pair of students. Add extra ideas to your own brainstorm if you need to.

analysis

  5

Now think about the colours used in the *Spider-Man* film. What colours are associated with particular characters? These could be the colours of their clothes, but they might also be colours in their surroundings – on the walls, fittings and furniture in the place where they live. Consider what these colours suggest about the characters.

Sound

 1 hour

Information

Types of sound in films

Sound is crucial for making a film believable and for creating mood and meaning. Dialogue and sound effects enable audiences to make sense of what is happening, helping to create the feeling of being present at the action. Sounds can be related to action within the frame and can also be heard from 'outside' it, for example doorbells ringing, traffic sounds and people's voices.

Here are some of the main types of sound you can hear in films:

★ Diegetic sound (sound within the film's world)

This is everything you would expect to hear as you watch the visuals. It includes dialogue; any music produced from something within the film, such as a radio; noise, such as footsteps, made by the characters themselves; and incidental noises such as telephones ringing or doors opening.

★ Non-diegetic sound (sound added to the film's world)

This is sound added in the studio during editing. It includes background music, voiceovers, sudden noises for special effects or any type of amplified sound.

Music is the main non-diegetic element of sound in films and it is crucial for creating the mood and atmosphere in each scene. Individual characters frequently have musical themes associated with them. Listen to the love theme in *Spider-Man* that features in some of the scenes with Peter Parker and MJ. Consider how this music encourages the audience to empathise with Peter's predicament as circumstances often prevent him from revealing his love for her.

★ Silence

Directors sometimes use no sound at all to create a dramatic or tense atmosphere, often just before something threatening or sinister happens to a character.

★ Sound bridges

These can be created through dialogue, music or other sound effects that continue into new scenes even after the visual images of the previous scene have ended. Conversely, the sound from the next scene sometimes begins before the current scene is concluded. Sound bridges can create a sense of continuity in films by making a smooth transition between scenes. Without bridges, the film can feel disjointed.

analysis

6 In pairs, watch the following chapters and scenes several times and make notes on how the director uses sound to create mood and atmosphere or to help advance the story. Share the workload by dividing between you the types of sound that you will listen out for.

★ Chapter 1, Start (Begin just at the end of the opening credits and the introduction of the bus scene.)

★ Chapter 13, Chasing Uncle Ben's killer.

 7 Spend a few minutes comparing and updating your notes with your partner before engaging in the whole-class discussion. Whether you have a whole-class discussion after each scene or discuss both scenes together will be at the discretion of your teacher. Focus your discussion on the following questions:

★ Which kinds of sound were most important in the chapters and scenes that you watched?

★ How did sound help to set the mood and atmosphere of the scenes?

★ Was the story advanced in any way by the use of sound?

★ Did you note any special devices such as sound bridges? If so, how and why were they used?

The camera

 1–2 hours

! Information

Camera shots and angles

The way shots are framed – their size, angle and distance – can have a direct bearing on the narrative and on how the audience react to what they see.

Directors often shoot scenes with several cameras and then select a wide variety of shots to build the visual story. There are many different types of camera shot; here are some of the main ones:

★ Establishing shot or long shot (ES or LS) – the subject is at a distance from a camera. This establishes the location and occasionally the time too. Sometimes directors use a re-establishing shot at the end of a scene to remind the audience of a scene's location.

★ Total shot (TS) – a head-to-toe shot, usually with the purpose of introducing significant characters in a scene.

★ Medium shot (MU) – generally focuses on a character from knees or waist up; often used to show relationships between two characters in a scene.

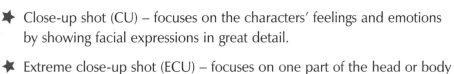

- ✦ Close-up shot (CU) – focuses on the characters' feelings and emotions by showing facial expressions in great detail.

- ✦ Extreme close-up shot (ECU) – focuses on one part of the head or body and can highlight emotions such as anger, joy, anxiety or fear.

- ✦ Point of view shot (POV) – shows a scene from a character's point of view.

- ✦ High angle shot – looks down on a character and makes them appear vulnerable. This can also be a point of view shot scene through the eyes of a more powerful character.

- ✦ Low angle shot – looks up at a character or object to make them appear more powerful or threatening.

- ✦ Two and three shots – two or more characters appearing in the same frame.

Combining camera shots

Many of these shots can be combined to achieve various effects. For example, in Chapter 7, during the fight between Peter Parker and Flash, Peter flips over and the audience momentarily suddenly sees things from Peter's point of view as he looks up at the faces of the surrounding crowd. This shot combines both low angle and point of view to give the audience Peter's bewildered perspective in this unusual fight scene.

Other combination shots include:

- ✦ Over the shoulder shot – usually a close-up or mid shot over a character's shoulder. It enables the audience to get an intimate view of a conversation and to identify with a character.

- ✦ Reaction shots – often short close-ups or mid shots to catch the reaction of a character to something that has just happened or been said. Reaction shots help to give a feeling of real-life human interaction and thus bring a sense of reality to a scene.

The next two pages show the story of Harry Palmer, the apparently bumbling employee of MaxSoft Inc., but secretly Z-Man, scourge of all New York villains.

comprehension

8 Identify the camera shots in the storyboard and explain the purpose behind each one.

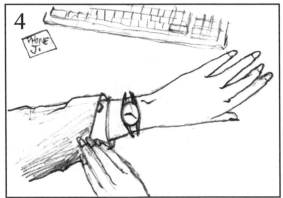

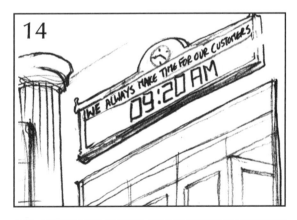

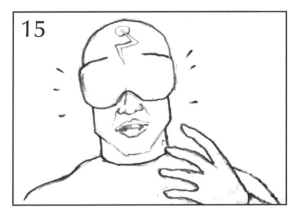

Narrative and representation in Spider-Man

9 Agree your answers with a partner and amend your own answers if necessary. Return to the Information box on camera shots and angles if you need to reread and clarify any information on this topic.

Information

Narrative patterns of camera shots

As you would expect, camera shots are not thrown together randomly. If you look carefully you will notice patterns of camera shots that help bring the action to a climax and then let it down again. For instance, a common narrative pattern found in TV as well as film unfolds as follows:

1 An establishing shot or long shot (as a kind of shorthand to show where the scene is taking place)

2 One or more total shots to introduce the characters that will be important in the scene

3 Several mid shots as characters talk to one another

4 Several close-ups to show anger or another emotion to produce an emotional climax or suspense

5 Several mid shots as the tension or drama lessens

6 One or two total shots to show characters leaving a room, building, etc.

7 Sometimes a re-establishing shot to remind the audience of the scene's location.

10 Stories in films and comics follow a similar narrative structure and this is especially true when a film is derived from a comic.

In an interview, *Spider-Man*'s director, Sam Raimi, said that he learned how to frame camera shots by studying superhero comics like *Spider-Man*. Several poses that Spider-Man strikes in the film are directly taken from the original Marvel comics.

Get a copy of any modern superhero comic published by Marvel and select a story to study. Alternatively, find some storyboards at the website below. Practise identifying camera shots and then explain their effectiveness.

Resources 4

This website on the film has lots of pictures, at least two early drafts of the script and, most importantly, early storyboards that you can use for spotting camera shots, angles, etc.
http://spideymovie.20m.com/

Camera movement

 1 hour

Information

Just as camera shots are framed to help audiences interpret a film's narrative, so camera movement can direct an audience's attention to details or to a particular viewpoint within a film.

In the early days of film-making, scenes were shot with only one or two cameras positioned on fixed tripods, so that reality appeared in a rather two-dimensional way. Now, camera movement and the use of multiple cameras mean that audience can see the action from multiple perspectives, giving a more realistic experience.

The main types of camera movement that you will see in films can be found on Worksheet 27.

analysis

 11 Watch the scene in Chapter 8, Scaling the heights, in which Peter discovers his ability to climb walls and jump great distances as he leaps from one building to another. The director uses several types of camera movement in this scene. Try to spot as many camera movements as you can and explain their purposes.

Watch the scene a few times then confer with your partner as you write up your notes.

evaluation

 12 Check your ideas in a brief whole-class discussion to review camera movement. Add to your notes any ideas that you had not thought of before that arise out of the discussion.

! Information

Why edit a film?

Film directors and editors splice scenes together in the way that they think will form the most effective and compact narrative for their films. Not all the filmed footage is used – some scenes are deleted for the sake of time or economy. The scenes that end up in the finished film show precisely what their directors want them to show. For example, Sam Raimi includes just enough family scenes of Peter Parker with his aunt and uncle to show how Peter's relationship with them alters as he becomes more aware of his new powers. If the director had added more scenes he would have risked boring his audience by slowing the pace of the narrative.

How camera cuts help a film's continuity and flow

The cuts should help the flow and continuity of a film's storyline(s). The types of cuts that directors insert between scenes are very important because these act as cues for audiences, helping them to pick up the storyline quickly and easily. Notice also that the number of cuts affects the speed of the editing. When Peter Parker jumps from one building to another the rapid editing helps reflect his feelings about his new found powers. Some of the most common types of cut used are set out below.

Type of cut	What it looks like	Its purpose
Straight cut	Hardly noticeable – like the blink of an eye.	This is the most common type of cut and normally borders long takes (holding shots). It maintains the flow of the narrative and sews the story together in a seamless way. Straight cuts are also used for cutaway shots that *briefly* show another location away from the main take, such as a crowd or characters away from the main action. For instance, the camera could hold a long take on a ticking bomb in a bank and cutaway for a brief shot of a crowd unaware in the street.

Type of cut	What it looks like	Its purpose
Dissolve	One image appears beneath another.	The idea is to blend closely from related scenes. They can also show a lapse of time or begin and end characters' flashbacks.
Fade in/out	The screen darkens or lightens before the next image (and scene) fills the screen.	Often indicates a movement in time, a new location or another story within the main narrative. Fades can also point to the end of an episode in a film.
Wipe cut	A new scene is introduced by one part of the screen wiping away the old scene.	This cut is used in comedies or action adventure films to introduce new locations or storylines. Several examples can be seen in Chapter 14, 'Spider-Man to the rescue', where the public are interviewed about Spider-Man. This type of cut suits the comic-book genre of the film.
Jump cut	The camera shot jumps within a scene to someone or something.	This makes the audience focus suddenly on a character or prop.
Montage	A number of brief shots follow in close succession.	Montage can give a lot of information in a brief period of time. For an example in *Spider-Man*, look again at the end of Chapter 8 where Peter Parker designs his costume for the wrestling match.

analysis

13 Examine the opening of any feature film and try to work out how the director manipulates the camera to achieve various effects. See if you can identify any of the cuts described above. A good film to try is Baz Luhrmann's *Romeo and Juliet* (1996). Work in pairs and replay the opening of the film as many times as you need to write your notes.

14 Discuss the film opening that you selected and explain to the class the range and purpose of edits in the opening scenes. Add to your notes any interesting comments made by others.

Mise en scène

 Information

This is a term that comes from the French and means literally 'put on stage'. It refers to the way each scene is composed as if it were a painting:

★ the characters' appearance including costumes, make-up, hairstyles, acting styles and props

★ the actors' facial expressions and body language

★ lighting and colour

★ the settings and props

★ how objects and characters are positioned within a frame

★ the camera distances and angles.

Everything that you see in a film scene is carefully selected to create an atmosphere, reveal a character and build upon the audience's expectations that arise out of a film's genre.

15 Explore the idea of *mise en scène* by studying the still opposite from *The Age of Innocence* and answering the questions below. Many of the questions do not necessarily have a 'correct' answer and there will often be scope for debate. Nevertheless, try to arrive at answers based on solid reasoning.

✦ What do you think is going on in this still or has happened prior to it?

✦ What kind of place is this?

✦ Where does this scene take place?

✦ When do you think it was set?

✦ How do you know when it takes place?

✦ Who is the key character in this scene and how do you know this? (Think about positioning within the frame, lighting and colour, eyelines, camera angles, distance, etc.)

✦ What is the mood of this still and how is it conveyed? (Think about body language, facial expressions, lighting, colour, etc.)

✦ What is the audience expected to make of the characters in this scene?

✦ Judging by the appearance of the characters and props, what would you say is the film's genre?

Resources 5

For extra help and advice try either of these websites.

Try the concept button at *Film Education* for more information on *mise en scène* and other film language. You will also find a range of resources that will be helpful for other parts of this challenge.
http://www.filmeducation.org/

CINEMATOGRAPHICAL & FILM PRODUCTION TERMS
http://www.theblackbook.net/acad/tagg/teaching/mmi/filmtrms.html

16 Discuss your answers in a whole-class session. Clarify your ideas by asking questions and add to your written answers where necessary.

Finally, you will need to review your understanding of *mise en scène* and all the other film techniques and conventions that you studied before you go on to tackle the next part of this challenge.

1 Watch the *Spider-Man* DVD, Chapter 17, World Unity Festival, and Chapter 18, Battle over Times Square, and write a short essay about how the director presents these scenes.

View the scenes several times and each time write notes on a separate aspect of film language. You can save some time by pairing up with another student and writing your notes together. This would also be a good way of checking your ideas.

When you have completed your notes, you should make a plan before drafting your essay. You should write a first draft before going on to produce your best draft. Remember also that the second draft is an opportunity to improve upon the first both in content and expression.

evaluation

2 Discuss some of the essays in class. There is no need to read out all of them; you might, for example, make a contribution on a particular aspect of film language, reading just the relevant part of your work. Your teacher and other students may comment on your points. Alternative interpretations and unusual contributions will add spice and breadth to the discussion. You will be able to sharpen your analytical skills by trying out your ideas on others.

F

Film critics

3–4 hours

application

1 Choose an activity and then present your completed work to the class. The activity will enable you to demonstrate your knowledge in a creative way. You could choose one that suits your intelligence and learning style best, or you could also boost another intelligence by trying a different activity.

Visual-linguistic task

★ Study the first few minutes of a film of your choice, then write an analysis. (It is best to stick to a short excerpt of approximately 5 minutes, because your analysis will be much more detailed than if you try to analyse an entire film.) In the introduction to your essay, however, you could sum up what is happening and write about the film's main themes (messages and ideas) and characters.

When you present your work to the class, explain your choice of film. and read a few selected highlights or summarise the main discoveries that you made whilst analysing the film.

Visual-spatial tasks

★ Create an information display to help Year 9 students understand some aspects of film language. Use *Spider-Man* or another film as the focus for your display. Do not attempt to explain all the aspects – choose the ones that are most relevant to the film that you are using for your focus. If you use *Spider-Man* you could also include information on:

- how the superhero is represented in comic books and the film

- how Peter Parker's character develops in the film

- how other characters form a contrast with Peter

- the film's main themes.

Think carefully about the best ways to represent each type of information. When you present your work to the class, give reasons for your choice of film and explain the aims of your display.

★ Storyboard a scene for a film about a superhero of your choice. You should include the following to make your work authentic:

- commonly found themes and storylines

- typical comic-book characters, including well-known villains

- speech/script

- film language (advice on how the shots should look and the kinds of sound/SFX that can accompany the shots).

Resources 6

For help with this task you should look again at storyboards on the Internet. Comics are another good source of ideas.

This is a good interactive website that you can use to practise writing storyboards:
http://www.plugincinema.com/plugin/film_school/interactive.html

Auditory task

★ One helpful feature on a DVD is that you can record your own commentary on the film on a PC.

Select two or more chapters from the film and produce a commentary on some of the following points in your chosen scenes:

- how the superhero is represented in comic books and in the film

- how Peter Parker's character develops in the film

- how other characters form a contrast with Peter

- the film's main themes

- significant use of film language

- your own ideas on your selected scenes.

If you would like to try this task with a different film, you could tape your ideas with the sound of the video or DVD turned down. The bullet points can be adapted for the film you choose. When presenting your work to the class, play your tape or give a live oral presentation running in sync with the video or DVD.

Remember that you will need to do some trial runs before you can give a confident oral presentation in conjunction with the film recording.

Kinaesthetic tasks

If your school has a suitable camera and editing equipment, you could write and produce a short film. You could pair up or form a group with like-minded students and try one of the following.

★ Film a superhero story from a comic book in several long takes with various kinds of cuts for each image from the comic. You could then dub a director's commentary on the images, explaining the type of shot, angle, theme, storyline, characteristics of the superhero, etc. Show your film to the class and field questions on what you did and how you achieved it.

★ Plan and produce a short documentary on how a famous fictional character like Harry Potter, Batman or Frodo Baggins translates to the big screen. You could have a number of talking heads speaking about the themes, characters and film language in the chosen film. You could also show a film clip or two taken from videos or DVDs to reinforce and illustrate your points after your presentation.

For further ideas, view some of the DVD's features on the making of *Spider-Man* and the problems that the film-makers had in translating it from comic books to the big screen.

Resources 7

Useful technical advice on how to storyboard and shoot your film using a video can be found at *The Challenge 2000 Multimedia Project*. Click the heading *Curriculum and Activities*.
http://pblmm.k12.ca.us/index.html

If you are using Apple Mac iMovie software to edit your film, the *University of Stevenson* website below has lots of very useful links to help you make the most of your equipment:
http://www4.district125.k12.il.us/webmeisters/cchausis/tutorial/imovie.html

evaluation

 2

Spend some time discussing each other's contributions. Share ideas and point out where improvements or different interpretations could be made. The feedback from other students will be useful for evaluating your work on this task and for considering your success on the assignment as a whole.

G · Learning review

 15 minutes

evaluation

 1

Fill in the assessment grid and add it to the notes and work from this assignment that you already have in your portfolio.

WS 31

How confident are you that you achieved the aims of this challenge?

Aim achieved	Not very confident	Reasonably confident	Confident	Very confident
I know how superheroes are represented in comic books and films.				
I understand character development and the main themes of *Spider-Man*.				

continued overleaf

Aim achieved	Not very confident	Reasonably confident	Confident	Very confident
I was able to see and explain how the director used key elements of film language.				
I was able to demonstrate my knowledge of film language in an analytical or creative way.				

Next steps

You could develop your knowledge of film by comparing two films from the action–adventure genre. Good choices for this comparative study could include:

★ any film in the James Bond series

★ *The Mummy* (either film)

★ any film from the *Indiana Jones* series

★ any film from the *Lord of The Rings* series.

You could compare:

★ the characteristics of the central characters, including the villains

★ the representation of women

★ the use of settings and locations

★ the use of film language

★ the action (chase sequences, fights, etc.)

★ time and technology including SFX.

After viewing the two films it would then be a good idea to select either the opening sequence or two other scenes from each and concentrate your analysis and comments on those.

You could also extend your knowledge of film language by visiting this website on film terms:
http://www.aber.ac.uk/media/Documents/short/gramtv.html

Detectives and murder mystery

Target

This challenge will enable you to:

★ understand the genre and conventions of crime fiction

★ develop deductive reasoning skills by studying Sherlock Holmes' methods of observation and deduction in Sir Arthur Conan Doyle's story, *A Study in Scarlet*

★ apply your detective skills to a murder mystery text

★ show your understanding of murder mysteries by writing a murder mystery story or planning and producing a game.

About this assignment

This assignment links to other subjects in the curriculum. Your work may incorporate:

★ drama

★ media

★ music

★ ICT

★ science

Learning styles

For each activity, consider how you might work in the learning style that suits you best:

★ auditory   ★ kinaesthetic   ★ visual   ★ any combination of these.

A   *Definitions and types of detectives*   *1 hour*

knowledge

    1

Before you begin studying murder mystery texts, check your understanding of the subject matter. Research and make notes on the following.

★ Define the term 'detective'.

★ Write a list of synonyms for 'detective' and make a note of whether each would be used in Britain or the United States.

★ What is the difference between a police detective and a private investigator/detective? What kind of crimes does each aim to solve?

2 With a partner, brainstorm a list of famous detectives from literature, television and the cinema. Then choose one detective from your list – perhaps the one you like most – and write a profile for them. The profile should include:

★ the detective's full name, sex and approximate age

★ where they live (type of home, the town and the country)

★ the name of their partner or associate

★ the detective's favoured type of transport

★ the type of crime they usually solve

★ their favoured method of solving crimes

★ marital status

★ financial situation

★ style of dress

★ private interests or hobbies

★ the detective's reputation among other characters

★ any ways in which the detective could be considered to be 'an outsider' or different from other people

★ any other aspects of the detective's character not yet mentioned

★ the reason you chose this detective for your profile.

evaluation

3 In a whole-class discussion, check your answers for question 1, then compare your detective profiles, making notes on the main similarities and differences. These will help you to gain an understanding of the detective fiction genre.

B *How does television murder mystery fit the genre?*

2–3 *hours*

Information

Types of murder mystery

The plot in a murder mystery story is usually one of two types:

★ a 'whodunit?', in which the detective (and the audience) do not know the identity of the murderer. The detective collects and assesses clues and weighs the alibis and motives of the suspects. Sometimes the detective assembles all the suspects at the end and unmasks the murderer, explaining how the dark deed was carried out. Only at that point do the audience find out whether they have arrived at the correct solution. Agatha Christie's detective, Hercule Poirot, always solves 'whodunits'.

✦ a 'how done it?', in which the detective knows the identity of the murderer but needs to prove it. The audience gradually discovers how the murder was carried out as the detective unravels the clues. Columbo, the detective from the US television series of the same name, usually solves 'how done its'.

Some fictional detectives are associated with both types of plots.

The main conventions in a murder mystery
Murder mystery stories usually include the following conventions:

✦ scene of the crime

✦ victim(s)

✦ criminal(s)

✦ suspects, including 'a least likely' suspect

✦ the detective, who is very often 'an outsider'

✦ clues, including 'red herrings'

✦ mystery

✦ justice.

Other conventions found in many stories of this genre include:

✦ an unusual murder

✦ a locked room

✦ suspense

✦ witnesses and witness statements

✦ motives

✦ alibis

✦ confessions

✦ a reconstruction of the crime

✦ a final twist in the plot.

1 Watch an episode of a murder mystery programme on television that features a well-known detective. Write notes in either linear or spidergram form on your chosen programme. Include the following details:

✦ the name of the programme and the detective

✦ the type of plot (is it a 'how done it' or 'whodunit'?)

✦ a brief summary of the plot

✦ the name and background of the victim and how they were murdered

✦ details of the crime scene

✦ the names and backgrounds of the suspects and the killer

✦ their alibis

✦ key witnesses

✦ the killer's motive(s)

✦ clues and red herrings

✦ the steps the detective took to solve the crime

✦ the main sources of mystery and suspense.

evaluation

 2 Talk about your programme in a whole-class discussion. Consider the similarities and differences between the detectives studied and the plots usually associated with them. Note down any new ideas on the genre or anything unusual or noteworthy about the stories discussed.

⭐ C *A study of* A Study in Scarlet   *2–3 hours*

knowledge

 1 Read the following extract from *A Study in Scarlet*, the first ever Sherlock Holmes story by Sir Arthur Conan Doyle.

> **From a window of his rooms overlooking Baker Street, Sherlock Holmes observes a messenger checking door numbers on the other side of the street; Holmes tells his sceptical new room mate and fellow observer, Watson, that the messenger is "a retired sergeant from the marines".**

The messenger eventually finds 221b and delivers a note to Holmes. Watson is staggered to learn from the messenger that he had indeed been a sergeant in the marines and that his usual commissionaire's uniform was at the cleaners. Nevertheless, Watson is still not fully convinced of Holmes' powers of observation nor his skills in "the science of deduction".

A Study in Scarlet, Chapter 3.

The Lauriston Gardens Mystery

I confess that I was considerably startled by this fresh proof of the practical nature of my companion's theories. My respect for his powers of analysis increased wondrously. There still remained some lurking suspicion in my mind, however, that the whole thing was a prearranged episode, intended to dazzle me, though what earthly object he could have in taking me in was past my comprehension. When I looked at him he had finished reading the note, and his eyes had assumed the vacant, lack-lustre expression which showed mental abstraction.

'How in the world did you deduce that?' I asked.

'Deduce what?' said he, petulantly.

'Why, that he was a retired sergeant of Marines.'

'I have no time for trifles,' he answered, brusquely; then with a smile, 'Excuse my rudeness. You broke the thread of my thoughts; but perhaps it is as well. So you actually were not able to see that that man was a sergeant of Marines?'

'No, indeed.'

'It was easier to know it than to explain why I know it. If you were asked to prove that two and two made four, you might find some difficulty, and yet you are quite sure of the fact. Even across the street I could see a great blue anchor tattooed on the back of the fellow's hand. That smacked of the sea. He had a military carriage, however, and regulation side whiskers. There we have the marine. He was a man with some amount of self-importance and a certain air of command. You must have observed the way in which he held his head and swung his cane. A steady, respectable, middle-aged man, too, on the face of him—all facts which led me to believe that he had been a sergeant.'

'Wonderful!' I ejaculated.

'Commonplace,' said Holmes, though I thought from his expression that he was pleased at my evident surprise and admiration. 'I said just now that there were no criminals. It appears that I am wrong—look at this!' He threw me over the note which the commissionaire had brought.'

'Why,' I cried, as I cast my eye over it, 'this is terrible!'

'It does seem to be a little out of the common,' he remarked, calmly. 'Would you mind reading it to me aloud?'

This is the letter which I read to him:

My Dear Mr. Sherlock Holmes,

There has been a bad business during the night at 3, Lauriston Gardens, off the Brixton Road. Our man on the beat saw a light there about two in the morning, and as the house was an empty one, suspected that something was amiss. He found the door open, and in the front room, which is bare of furniture, discovered the body of a gentleman, well dressed, and having cards in his pocket bearing the name of 'Enoch J. Drebber, Cleveland, Ohio, U.S.A.' There had been no robbery, nor is there any evidence as to how the man met his death. There are marks of blood in the room, but there is no wound upon his person. We are at a loss as to how he came into the empty house; indeed, the whole affair is a puzzler. If you can come round to the house any time before twelve, you will find me there. I have left everything *in statu quo* until I hear from you. If you are unable to come I shall give you fuller details, and would esteem it a great kindness if you would favour me with your opinion.

Yours faithfully,
Tobias Gregson

'Gregson is the smartest of the Scotland Yarders,' my friend remarked; 'he and Lestrade are the pick of a bad lot. They are both quick and energetic, but conventional—shockingly so. They have their knives into one another, too. They are as jealous as a pair of professional beauties. There will be some fun over this case if they are both put upon the scent.'

I was amazed at the calm way in which he rippled on. 'Surely there is not a moment to be lost,' I cried, 'shall I go and order you a cab?'

'I'm not sure about whether I shall go. I *am* the most incurably lazy devil that ever stood in shoe leather—that is, when the fit is on me, for I can be spry enough at times.'

'Why, it is just such a chance as you have been longing for.'

'My dear fellow, what does it matter to me. Supposing I unravel the whole matter, you may be sure that Gregson, Lestrade, and Co. will pocket all the credit. That comes of being an unofficial personage.'

'But he begs you to help him.'

'Yes. He knows that I am his superior, and acknowledges it to me; but he would cut his tongue out before he would own it to any third person. However, we may as well go and have a look. I shall work it out on my own hook. I may have a laugh at them, if I have nothing else. Come on!'

He hustled on his overcoat, and bustled about in a way that showed that an energetic fit had superseded the apathetic one.

'Get your hat,' he said.

'You wish me to come?'

'Yes, if you have nothing better to do.' A minute later we were both in a hansom, driving furiously for the Brixton Road.

It was a foggy, cloudy morning, and a dun-coloured veil hung over the house-tops, looking like the reflection of the mud-coloured streets beneath. My companion was in the best of spirits, and prattled away about Cremona fiddles, and the difference between a Stradivarius and an Amati. As for myself, I was silent, for the dull weather and the melancholy business upon which we were engaged, depressed my spirits.

'You don't seem to give much thought to the matter in hand,' I said at last, interrupting Holmes' musical disquisition.

Peter Cushing starred as Sherlock Holmes in many films and a television series based on Sir Arthur Conan Doyle's famous detective.

'No data yet,' he answered. 'It is a capital mistake to theorize before you have all the evidence. It biases the judgment.'

'You will have your data soon,' I remarked, pointing with my finger; ' this is the Brixton Road, and that is the house, if I am not very much mistaken.'

'So it is. Stop, driver, stop!' We were still a hundred yards or so from it, but he insisted upon our alighting, and we finished our journey upon foot.

Number 3, Lauriston Gardens wore an ill-omened and minatory look. It was one of four which stood back some little way from the street, two being occupied and two empty. The latter looked out with three tiers of vacant melancholy windows, which were blank and dreary, save that here and there a 'To Let' card had developed like a cataract upon the bleared panes. A small garden sprinkled over with a scattered eruption of sickly plants separated each of these houses from the street, and was traversed by a narrow pathway, yellowish in colour, and consisting apparently of a mixture of clay and of gravel. The whole place was very sloppy from the rain which had fallen through the night. The garden was bounded by a three-foot brick wall with a fringe of wood rails upon the top, and against this wall was leaning a stalwart police constable, surrounded by a small knot of loafers, who craned their necks and strained their eyes in the vain hope of catching some glimpse of the proceedings within.

I had imagined that Sherlock Holmes would at once have hurried into the house and plunged into a study of the mystery. Nothing appeared to be further from his intention. With an air of nonchalance which, under the circumstances, seemed to me to border upon affectation, he lounged up and down the pavement, and gazed vacantly at the ground, the sky, the opposite houses and the line of railings. Having finished his scrutiny, he proceeded slowly down the path, or rather down the fringe of grass which flanked the path, keeping his eyes riveted upon the ground. Twice he stopped, and once I saw him smile, and heard him utter an exclamation of satisfaction. There were many marks of footsteps upon the wet clayey soil; but since the police had been coming and going over it, I was unable to see how my companion could hope to learn anything from it. Still I had had such extraordinary evidence of the quickness of his perceptive faculties, that I had no doubt that he could see a great deal which was hidden from me.

At the door of the house we were met by a tall, white-faced, flaxen-haired man, with a notebook in his hand, who rushed forward and wrung my companion's hand with effusion. 'It is indeed kind of you to come,' he said, 'I have had everything left untouched.'

'Except that!' my friend answered, pointing at the pathway. 'If a herd of buffaloes had passed along there could not be a greater mess. No doubt, however, you had drawn your own conclusions, Gregson, before you permitted this.'

'I have had so much to do inside the house,' the detective said evasively. 'My colleague, Mr. Lestrade, is here. I had relied upon him to look after this.'

Holmes glanced at me and raised his eyebrows sardonically. 'With two such men as yourself and Lestrade upon the ground, there will not be much for a third party to find out,' he said.

Gregson rubbed his hands in a self-satisfied way. 'I think we have done all that can be done,' he answered; 'it's a queer case though, and I knew your taste for such things.'

'You did not come here in a cab?' asked Sherlock Holmes.

'No, sir.'

'Nor Lestrade?'

'No, sir.'

'Then let us go and look at the room.' With which inconsequent remark he strode on into the house, followed by Gregson, whose features expressed his astonishment.

A short passage, bare-planked and dusty, led to the kitchen and offices. Two doors opened out of it to the left and to the right. One of these had obviously been closed for many weeks. The other belonged to the dining-room, which was the apartment in which the mysterious affair had occurred. Holmes walked in, and I followed him with that subdued feeling at my heart which the presence of death inspires.

It was a large square room, looking all the larger from the absence of all furniture. A vulgar flaring paper adorned the walls, but it was blotched in places with mildew, and here and there great strips had become detached and hung down, exposing the yellow plaster beneath.

Opposite the door was a showy fireplace, surmounted by a mantelpiece of imitation white marble. On one corner of this was stuck the stump of a red wax candle. The solitary window was so dirty that the light was hazy and uncertain, giving a dull grey tinge to everything, which was intensified by the thick layer of dust which coated the whole apartment.

All these details I observed afterwards. At present my attention was centred upon the single grim motionless figure which lay stretched upon the boards, with vacant sightless eyes staring up at the discoloured ceiling. It was that of a man about forty-three or forty-four years of age, middle-sized, broad-shouldered, with crisp curling black hair, and a short stubbly beard. He was dressed in a heavy broadcloth frock coat and waistcoat, with light-coloured trousers, and immaculate collar and cuffs. A top hat, well brushed and trim, was placed upon the floor beside him. His hands were clenched and his arms thrown abroad, while his lower limbs were interlocked as though his death struggle had been a grievous one. On his rigid face there stood an expression of horror, and, as it seemed to me, of hatred, such as I have never seen upon human features. This malignant and terrible contortion, combined with the low forehead, blunt nose, and prognathous jaw, gave the dead man a singularly simous and ape-like appearance, which was increased by his writhing, unnatural posture. I have seen death in many forms, but never has it appeared to me in a more fearsome aspect than in that dark grimy apartment, which looked out upon one of the main arteries of suburban London.

Lestrade, lean and ferret-like as ever, was standing by the doorway, and greeted my companion and myself.

'This case will make a stir, sir,' he remarked. 'It beats anything I have seen, and I am no chicken.'

'There is no clue?' said Gregson.

'None at all,' chimed in Lestrade.

Sherlock Holmes approached the body, and, kneeling down, examined it intently. 'You are sure that there is no wound?' he asked, pointing to numerous gouts and splashes of blood which lay all round.

'Positive!' cried both detectives.

'Then, of course, this blood belongs to a second individual—presumably the murderer, if murder has been committed. It reminds me of the

circumstances attendant on the death of Van Jansen, in Utrecht, in the year '34. Do you remember the case, Gregson?'

'No, sir.'

'Read it up—you really should. There is nothing new under the sun. It has all been done before.'

As he spoke, his nimble fingers were flying here, there, and everywhere, feeling, pressing, unbuttoning, examining, while his eyes wore the same far-away expression which I have already remarked upon. So swiftly was the examination made, that one would hardly have guessed the minuteness with which it was conducted. Finally, he sniffed the dead man's lips, and then glanced at the soles of his patent leather boots.

'He has not been moved at all?' he asked.

'No more than was necessary for the purposes of our examination.'

'You can take him to the mortuary now,' he said. 'There is nothing more to be learned.'

Gregson had a stretcher and four men at hand. At his call they entered the room, and the stranger was lifted and carried out. As they raised him, a ring tinkled down and rolled across the floor. Lestrade grabbed it up and stared at it with mystified eyes.

'There's been a woman here,' he cried. 'It's a woman's wedding-ring.'

He held it out, as he spoke, upon the palm of his hand. We all gathered round him and gazed at it. There could be no doubt that that circlet of plain gold had once adorned the finger of a bride.

'This complicates matters,' said Gregson. 'Heaven knows, they were complicated enough before.'

'You're sure it doesn't simplify them?' observed Holmes. 'There's nothing to be learned by staring at it. What did you find in his pockets?'

'We have it all here,' said Gregson, pointing to a litter of objects upon one of the bottom steps of the stairs. 'A gold watch, No. 97163, by Barraud, of London. Gold Albert chain, very heavy and solid. Gold ring, with masonic device. Gold pin – bull-dog's head, with rubies as eyes. Russian leather card-case, with cards of Enoch J. Drebber of Cleveland, corresponding with the E. J. D. upon the linen. No purse, but loose money to the extent of seven pounds thirteen. Pocket edition of

Boccaccio's 'Decameron', with name of Joseph Stangerson upon the fly-leaf. Two letters – one addressed to E. J. Drebber and one to Joseph Stangerson.'

'At what address?'

'American Exchange, Strand – to be left till called for. They are both from the Guion Steamship Company, and refer to the sailing of their boats from Liverpool. It is clear that this unfortunate man was about to return to New York.'

'Have you made any inquiries as to this man, Stangerson?'

'I did it at once, sir,' said Gregson. 'I have had advertisements sent to all the newspapers, and one of my men has gone to the American Exchange, but he has not returned yet.'

'Have you sent to Cleveland?'

'We telegraphed this morning.'

'How did you word your inquiries?'

'We simply detailed the circumstances, and said that we should be glad of any information which could help us.'

'You did not ask for particulars on any point which appeared to you to be crucial?'

'I asked about Stangerson.'

'Nothing else? Is there no circumstance on which this whole case appears to hinge? Will you not telegraph again?'

'I have said all I have to say,' said Gregson, in an offended voice.

Sherlock Holmes chuckled to himself, and appeared to be about to make some remark, when Lestrade, who had been in the front room while we were holding this conversation in the hall, reappeared upon the scene, rubbing his hands in a pompous and self-satisfied manner.

'Mr. Gregson,' he said, 'I have just made a discovery of the highest importance, and one which would have been overlooked had I not made a careful examination of the walls.'

The little man's eyes sparkled as he spoke, and he was evidently in a state of suppressed exultation at having scored a point against his colleague.

'Come here,' he said, bustling back into the room, the atmosphere of which felt clearer since the removal of its ghastly inmate. 'Now, stand there!'

He struck a match on his boot and held it up against the wall.

'Look at that!' he said, triumphantly.

I have remarked that the paper had fallen away in parts. In this particular corner of the room a large piece had peeled off, leaving a yellow square of coarse plastering. Across this bare space there was scrawled in blood-red letters a single word—

Rache

'What do you think of that?' cried the detective, with the air of a showman exhibiting his show. 'This was overlooked because it was in the darkest corner of the room, and no one thought of looking there. The murderer has written it with his or her own blood. See this smear where it has trickled down the wall! That disposes of the idea of suicide anyhow. Why was that corner chosen to write it on? I will tell you. See that candle on the mantelpiece. It was lit at the time, and if it was lit this corner would be the brightest instead of the darkest portion of the wall.'

'And what does it mean now that you *have* found it?' asked Gregson in a depreciatory voice.

'Mean? Why, it means that the writer was going to put the female name Rachel, but was disturbed before he or she had time to finish. You mark my words, when this case comes to be cleared up you will find that a woman named Rachel has something to do with it. It's all very well for you to laugh, Mr. Sherlock Holmes. You may be very smart and clever, but the old hound is the best, when all is said and done.'

'I really beg your pardon!' said my companion, who had ruffled the little man's temper by bursting into an explosion of laughter. 'You certainly have the credit of being the first of us to find this out, and, as you say, it bears every mark of having been written by the other participant in last night's mystery. I have not had time to examine this room yet, but with your permission I shall do so now.'

As he spoke, he whipped a tape measure and a large round magnifying glass from his pocket. With these two implements he trotted noiselessly about the room, sometimes stopping, occasionally kneeling, and once

lying flat upon his face. So engrossed was he with his occupation that he appeared to have forgotten our presence, for he chattered away to himself under his breath the whole time, keeping up a running fire of exclamations, groans, whistles, and little cries suggestive of encouragement and of hope. As I watched him I was irresistibly reminded of a pure-blooded well-trained foxhound as it dashes backwards and forwards through the covert, whining in its eagerness, until it comes across the lost scent. For twenty minutes or more he continued his researches, measuring with the most exact care the distance between marks which were entirely invisible to me, and occasionally applying his tape to the walls in an equally incomprehensible manner. In one place he gathered up very carefully a little pile of grey dust from the floor, and packed it away in an envelope. Finally, he examined with his glass the word upon the wall, going over every letter of it with the most minute exactness. This done, he appeared to be satisfied, for he replaced his tape and his glass in his pocket.

'They say that genius is an infinite capacity for taking pains,' he remarked with a smile. 'It's a very bad definition, but it does apply to detective work.'

Gregson and Lestrade had watched the manoeuvres of their amateur companion with considerable curiosity and some contempt. They evidently failed to appreciate the fact, which I had begun to realise, that Sherlock Holmes' smallest actions were all directed towards some definite and practical end.

'What do you think of it, sir?' they both asked.

'It would be robbing you of the credit of the case if I was to presume to help you,' remarked my friend. 'You are doing so well now that it would be a pity for anyone to interfere.' There was a world of sarcasm in his voice as he spoke. 'If you will let me know how your investigations go,' he continued, 'I shall be happy to give you any help I can. In the meantime I should like to speak to the constable who found the body. Can you give me his name and address?'

Lestrade glanced at his note-book. 'John Rance,' he said. 'He is off duty now. You will find him at 46, Audley Court, Kennington Park Gate.'

Holmes took a note of the address.

'Come along, Doctor,' he said; 'we shall go and look him up. I'll tell you one thing which may help you in the case,' he continued, turning to the two detectives. 'There has been murder done, and the murderer was a man. He was more than six feet high, was in the prime of life, had small feet for his height, wore coarse, square-toed boots and smoked a Trichinopoly cigar. He came here with his victim in a four-wheeled cab, which was drawn by a horse with three old shoes and one new one on his off fore leg. In all probability the murderer had a florid face, and the finger-nails of his right hand were remarkably long. These are only a few indications, but they may assist you.'

Lestrade and Gregson glanced at each other with an incredulous smile.

'If this man was murdered, how was it done?' asked the former.

'Poison,' said Sherlock Holmes curtly, and strode off. 'One other thing, Lestrade,' he added, turning round at the door: ''Rache', is the German for 'revenge'; so don't lose your time looking for Miss Rachel.'

With which Parthian shot he walked away, leaving the two rivals open-mouthed behind him.

A Study In Scarlet, Chapter 3
Sir Arthur Conan Doyle

Resources 1

If you would like to read the whole text you may be able to find a copy at the school or local library.

Alternatively, go to the website below and click on the author A. C. Doyle. Then click *A Study in Scarlet*.
http://www.unityspot.com/arthurs/

analysis

 2

Now work through the text, sentence and word level questions. You do not have to answer every question, but make sure that you include some work at each level. Include notes on anything else that you find significant at text, sentence or word level that is not covered by any of the questions.

Text level

★ Summarise in about 100 words what happens in this chapter. (To do this you will need to select only the essential details.)

- Explain what you think is the writer's main aim or purpose in this chapter.

- Identify the genre of this text and explain how you know.

- Did you enjoy reading this chapter and would you choose to read this type of text for yourself?

Sentence level

- Who is the narrator of this text? Why do you think this type of narrator has been chosen?

- Read the Information box below, then select quotations from this chapter which show that Watson, quite ironically, is a keener observer than he claims to be, albeit in a literary sense. Look at the chapter again and scan for sentences and short passages where Watson makes observations on:

  - the weather during the journey to the crime scene

  - the atmosphere of the area where the crime takes place

  - the appearance and behaviour of Holmes, Lestrade and Gregson as well as the rivalry that exists between all three of them

  - the crime scene

  - the state of the victim.

  Write out three or four of the sentences and passages using quotation marks and explain what can be inferred from Watson's observations.

Information

Intelligences in Conan Doyle's characters

In Chapter 2 of *A Study in Scarlet*, Watson discovers that Holmes has large gaps in his knowledge. For instance, Holmes has hardly any literary knowledge at all because he is simply uninterested in literature; he is also unaware that the earth goes around the sun! Doctor Watson may not be skilled at the science of deduction, yet in a literary sense he is an excellent observer and keen reporter of what he sees. One could infer that the two characters rely on different intelligences. Holmes uses visual-spatial intelligence; he is also strong in kinaesthetic and auditory intelligences as well as logic. Notice that he is quite oblivious to others as he moves around the crime scene, engrossed in his work, talking to himself and making encouraging 'whistles' and other noises! Watson, on the other hand, seems to use only one of his intelligences – his powerful visual-linguistic intelligence.

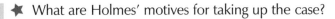

★ What are Holmes' motives for taking up the case?

★ The Information box below shows most of the techniques Sherlock Holmes employs in his 'science of deduction'. Reread the chapter and find at least six examples of deductive techniques used by Sherlock Holmes or by other characters. Write out each example with quotation marks and identify the type of technique in brackets.

Information

Deductive techniques

Observation	Using all five senses to pay close attention to everything that happens
Interpretation of data	Identifying relevant data and trends in data
Analysis	A careful examination of each element of the information
Hypothesising	Making a suggestion or proposition by reasoning from known facts
Use of variables	Exploring possibilities using 'if … then' statements
Prediction	Stating what may happen based on what you already know
Inference	Making a deduction or conclusion from observations and evidence
Organisation	Putting information in order
Classification	Putting information into classes or categories
Drawing conclusions	Summarising the data to answer the question stated in the problem

Resources 2

For more fascinating information on the science of deduction and Sherlock Holmes' creative thinking methods, go to the website *ThinkingCoach Online* and click on 'Sherlock Holmes'.
http://www.thinkingcoach.com/index.htm

Word level

★ Select words and phrases that Watson uses to create the mood and atmosphere of:

- the journey to the crime scene

- the area where the crime took place

- the crime scene

- the victim.

Briefly explain how each word or phrase contributes towards the mood and atmosphere of the chapter.

★ Watson says that he is 'irresistibly reminded of a pure-blooded well-trained foxhound' as he comtemplates Holmes at the crime scene. What can be inferred from this image?

★ The text is over 100 years old. Select a few unusual words or phrases from Chapter 3 that you think indicate the age of this text.

★ If you are unsure of the meaning of any of your selected words, find out their definitions. Consider how each word might be an appropriate choice for the text and the sentence where it occurs. Which words would you substitute as synonyms to enable a younger audience to understand this chapter?

evaluation

 3

Discuss each set of questions in class and add notes where necessary to add more detail to your answers. This is also an opportunity to clarify your ideas by asking questions and checking your answers with others. Revisit any aspect of the topic that you feel you need to research further before going on to the next task.

D *Could you be a detective?*   *6–7 hours*

application

1

Choose a murder mystery story or novel and try out your skills as a detective. You could choose one from the suggestions in the Help box, or another text agreed by your teacher. As you read, see how your skills of deduction compare with those of the detective in the story. Remember to be an active reader, making notes on your own deductions as you go along. Revisit the deductive techniques table to remind yourself of the different ways that you can think about the problem under investigation.

Help

You could choose a story or a novel from any of the following:

* the Sherlock Holmes series by Sir Arthur Conan Doyle
* the Nancy Drew series by various authors
* the Hercule Poirot mysteries by Agatha Christie
* the Miss Marple stories by Agatha Christie
* *The Moonstone* by Wilkie Collins
* the C. Auguste Dupin trilogy by Edgar Allan Poe.

Your teacher will give you plenty of quiet study time in class so you can read, concentrate and make notes. Produce linear or spidergram notes, using the following questions as a guide.

After the murder or at the scene of the crime

* Describe the appearance and character of the detective and partner (if they have one). What do you take to be their strengths and weaknesses?

* What does the detective make of the scene of the crime? What do you make of it? Make a note of any potentially significant or unusual details.

* List the clues as well as possible red herrings, and make an initial prediction of who you think will turn out to be the criminal.

During the investigation

* Identify the methods that the detective uses to investigate the crime. Decide whether you agree with their methods.

* Scan the 'data' for each witness and suspect and make notes on your own suspicions about the identity of the criminal.

* Explain what methods you have used to sift the clues or data to try and solve the crime.

* Resist the temptation to read on to discover the identity of the criminal! Use facts and evidence from your reading to try and solve the mystery for yourself.

At the end

* Write a brief summary of the plot, including any final twist. Explain what steps the detective has taken to solve the crime. (These could be done with bullet points.)

Detectives and murder mystery

★ Make a note of any other moral issues you think are significant, for example the treatment of women or ethnic minorities; the difference between rich and poor or the old and the young.

Resources 3

For excellent information on murder mystery writers try

A Guide to Classic Mystery and Detection
http://members.aol.com/MG4273/classics.htm

You can sharpen your skills in detection still further by attempting to solve one of the mini-mysteries on this fascinating website:

MysteryNet.com – the Online Mystery Network for everyone who enjoys a mystery
http://www.mysterynet.com/

evaluation

 2

Discuss the notes that you made about your novel or story with a group of other students. Pay attention to similarities and differences between the texts within the murder mystery genre. For instance, you could talk about the detectives, types of plots, murder mystery conventions, detective techniques, or moral issues.

Share your successes and failures in spotting the criminals and explain how you did it – or how you didn't! Make a mental note also of any recommendations for good reads.

 E *Create a murder mystery* 4–6 hours

application

 1

This activity will enable you to demonstrate your knowledge in a creative way. You may want to choose the activity that best suits your intelligence and learning style. Remember, however, that you can also build up another intelligence by trying a different type of activity. Never pass up a challenge – you should always aim to extend yourself as fully as you can.

Visual-linguistic task

Use your knowledge of the murder mystery genre to plan and write a story of your own. You could then read part of it to the class and discuss particular elements, for example the development of the plot and how your detective solved the case.

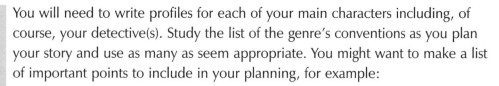

You will need to write profiles for each of your main characters including, of course, your detective(s). Study the list of the genre's conventions as you plan your story and use as many as seem appropriate. You might want to make a list of important points to include in your planning, for example:

- ✹ the characters (detective(s), suspects, witnesses and victim)

- ✹ the setting(s)

- ✹ the plot, possibly with a twist in the tale

- ✹ clues

- ✹ the detective's techniques

- ✹ justice

- ✹ the style of narration

- ✹ the structure – all the steps from the discovery of the crime to the unmasking of the criminal

- ✹ realistic dialogue

- ✹ description for characterisation and to set the scene and tone for mood, settings and atmosphere.

Remember to seed your plot with clues. Sherlock Holmes stories, for example, always include clues that enable the reader to solve the case – providing that they recognise their significance and can piece them all together.

Help

Finding ideas

A useful device for sparking ideas is to find a puzzling picture or photograph from a magazine, for example a photo of a person or a group of people staring at someone or something. Study the picture then invent some stories to explain what you see.

If you find that you cannot create a credible detective yourself, you could write a story about a fictional detective that you studied. If you decide to do this, you should try to imitate the writing style of the original stories. Look at some of the story titles that feature your detective as these may inspire you to think up a suitable story title of your own.

Visual-spatial, auditory and kinaesthetic tasks

If, like Sherlock Holmes you are comfortable using all of these intelligences, form a group with like-minded students and share the work of planning, writing and producing a murder mystery game. Then exchange games with another group and play one another's games.

You will need six to eight players or perhaps more, depending on the number of witnesses and suspects that you include in your game.

You will also need one of your group to play the host and oversee the game. This needs to be someone who is very familiar with the plot and all the roles being played. The groups can then play out the murder mystery games in front of an audience of non-participating students.

The game and its organisation may appear complicated, but it will not be difficult if you work through the following instructions step by step.

Help

How to plan and write a murder mystery game

1   Select a theme and title. Think carefully about the scope of any possible setting, for example a school reunion would allow you to create a number of characters from a range of occupations and backgrounds. For a newspaper office setting, on the other hand, you would have suspects and witnesses with occupations all related to newspapers and offices, for example reporters, editors, receptionists, the newspaper owner, photographers, copy-editors, cleaners, advertising sales people and security guards.

Some settings will automatically create a more structured format, which may make the game easier to run. For example you could have a coroner's inquest in which the host plays the coroner or a police officer. This will allow the host to introduce clues every 20 minutes or so or whenever the questioning of the suspects is running out of steam. A setting such as a party, ship or hotel means that no one is able to leave until they have been questioned.

You could choose any of the suggestions above or another theme – be as imaginative as you like!

2   Think about the crime. This could be a murder, or a theft of valuable or important property. Keep it down to just one murder or one theft. Any more will risk making the crime too complex and frustrating to solve.

3   Choose the victim. You could have a player taking the role, but remember that if the crime is a murder, that player will then miss most of

the action. In this case it is probably better to create an 'invisible' victim with the host explaining at the beginning of the game what happened.

4   Cast your characters as appropriately as you can. Ensure all the roles fit in with the themed setting.

5   Establish a number of motives for the theft or the murder. If the victim is a prominent member of that society or community, then the number of possible motives will probably be multiplied. Motives could include: ambition, blackmail, money, jealousy, job insecurity, infidelity and revenge.

6   Select the method of murder (poison, knife in the back, gunshot, etc.). You can be imaginative, but don't make it too complicated!

7   Write the plot. You need to plan where the crime will happen; at what time; what causes the murderer to act; whether the dying victim leaves a clue; what other clues might be found at the murder scene; what the murderer did afterwards.

8   Try to use about four main clues. At least one could be open to differing interpretations. (Remember the misinterpretations of 'Rache' in *A Study in Scarlet*.)

9   Create up to six main suspects. If you create too few, then the game becomes too easy; too many and the game will be too complicated.

10 Write an alibi for each of the suspects but remember to let the player know what really happened if the truth is different. It will be up to the other players to detect the false alibis.

11 Plan what information on each player will be given to which other players, for example one player may have some information on one or two of the other players. You should also decide whether one of the players has seen the murderer near the murder scene close to the time of the murder.

12 Prepare a set of information sheets or cards for each player. Present these as a pack in a plastic wallet. Each pack needs to include the following:

● the character's background. (Produce a profile for the character; you could also suggest a prop or a costume to add to the fun.)

● their alibi – where they were when the crime was committed and what they did afterwards. (They need to know *what* they did, *when* they did it and *the order* in which they did things.)

● their possible motives for having committed the crime (even if they are not the murderer)

● parts or all of the witness statement that they gave to the police

● *some* information on other suspects.

Try to make sure that each player receives exactly the information they should have about other players; there should be enough clues on the cards to enable the crime to be solved through intense questioning. Double check to see that you have not left any important pieces of information out!

Try to place *some* suspicion on all suspects, but not as heavily on the murderer. Give the murderer an alibi that is false but let the player know the truth. It will be up to the other players to see through the false alibi by using their skills of deduction.

Try not to introduce surprises that only one character knows. Make all information available to at least two characters.

Use the appropriate written form for each part of the information that you put on the players' cards. For instance, an autopsy can be written in a clinical, report style; your information on the other characters could be written informally in the second person (John Smith – you murdered Rachel Jones. You didn't mean to do so at first; but when you could see no end to her blackmail for more cash you simply snapped and killed her! Besides, you knew that she had almost bled you dry!) Whatever you write – be creative!

13 Prepare a pack for the host. This will need to include a summary of the crime divided into the following sections:

- the background and scene of the crime
- the evidence: wills, autopsy reports, forensic reports, witness statements, press clippings, etc.
- the main clues
- the solution
- a detailed timeline setting out the events around the murder.

Help

How to host and play a murder mystery game

To introduce the game, the host should narrate what has happened. If you like, you can recreate the crime scene with chalked lines and tomato ketchup!

Each suspect must tell their story separately and then field questions from other suspects/players. Suspects should reveal any clues they have and not hold back evidence from other players. They can, however, be devious in how they reveal evidence. Players do not have to follow the information sheets to the letter. They can lie or try to throw suspicion on other characters. It will depend on the other players using their questioning skills, to work out if they are telling the truth.

Do not worry about making minor mistakes as these can be useful and produce an even more enjoyable game.

The murderer can lie but will have to reveal the truth if cornered. Some of the murderer's details, such as the alibi, can be on one or two cards held by other players.

The host has the job of maintaining the flow of the game. In some settings, they can do this in role. For example in a coroner's inquest, they could act as senior police officer, directing matters and organising the questioning of witnesses and suspects. The host gradually releases the clues one by one during the progress of the game.

Once all of the evidence and clues have been revealed, the players should each make an accusation. The host can then announce who was correct by revealing the culprit's true identity and explaining how they did it.

You can adapt the game to suit your class. Make changes as you see fit for the game to work properly.

evaluation

 2 Review the successes or failures that you had in writing the story or planning, producing and playing the murder mystery game. Consider what changes you could make to improve the story or game. If you produced a game, you might think about how to make it workable for a younger or different set of players. Think about what you learned through the task and talk about what you did or did not enjoy about it.

F *Learning review* **20 minutes**

evaluation

 1 Fill in the assessment grid and add it to the notes and work from this assignment that you already have in your portfolio.

 How confident are you that you achieved the aims of this challenge?

Aim achieved	Not very confident	Reasonably confident	Confident	Very confident
I understand the genre and conventions of crime fiction.				
I improved my deductive reasoning skills by studying Sherlock Holmes' methods.				
I successfully applied my detective skills to a murder mystery text.				
I demonstrated my understanding of murder mysteries by writing a story or by producing and playing a game.				

WS 35

Next steps

You could take your work further with one or more of the following:

★ Compare two famous detectives created by different writers and write an essay on their similarities and differences.

★ Produce an information display for Year 7 on 'the science of deduction' illustrated with examples from a text.

★ Alter the format of your story or murder mystery game by changing part or all of it into a drama script. Write a report on the challenges and difficulties that you faced.